My NAME is
COOL

ANTONIO SACRE

My NAME is COOL

18 STORIES
FROM A CUBAN-IRISH-AMERICAN
STORYTELLER

Copyright © 2013 by Antonio Sacre

Published by Familius LLC, www.familius.com

Familius books are available at special discounts for bulk purchases for sales promotions, family or corporate use. Special editions, including personalized covers, excerpts of existing books, or books with corporate logos, can be created in large quantities for special needs. For more information, contact Premium Sales at 559-876-2170 or email specialmarkets@familius.com

Library of Congress Catalog-in-Publication Data

2013942247

pISBN 978-1-938301-56-8
eISBN 978-1-939629-02-9

Printed in the United States of America

Edited by Victoria Candland
Book design by David Miles
Cover and interior illustrations by Natalie Carter
Jacket design by David Miles

10 9 8 7 6 5 4 3

First Edition

Contents

TO OWEN JAMES

Prologue

*I*n 1960, my father got into a rowboat in Havana, Cuba, and rowed ninety miles to the United States to start his new life. By the time I was in the seventh grade, I was telling my friends that my father saved all of his family and all of his friends, piled everyone into that boat, and rowed everybody over to America. By the time I got into high school, I was telling my friends that my father stole five boats from Castro's navy and saved all of his friends, all of his family, all of his first, second, third, fourth, and fifth cousins, everyone on his block, all of the pets, and everybody on his baseball team. He piled them all into the boat. There was no room for him in the boat, so he tied those boats together with a big rope, put that rope around his shoulders, and swam everybody over to the United States.

When my dad heard that I was telling that story, he laughed. I said, "But really, you just came over in a boat with your family, right?"

He said, "Came over in a boat? What are you talking about? I flew over in a plane."

I said, "You didn't come over in a boat?"

He said, "No. You've been telling stories like that all your life."

And it's true, I have. Now, all these years later, it is my career and my calling. I write and tell stories primarily to entertain, but also, I hope, to shed some light on one tiny part of what it means to be the child of immigrants, or as my father says, "born in the United States with Cuban and Irish parts." Or as the late storyteller Pat Mendoza, a wonderful man with a perpetual smile, called me once while introducing me at the National Storytelling Festival, a "leprecano."

Here are the stories I have told, in forty-five states, in eight countries, for the past twenty years, to audiences of all ages.

SWIMMING WITH BARRACUDAS

A Storyteller's Simple History of Cuba

*I*f you've ever been to Disney World in Florida, you've been pretty close to Miami. And if you've been to Miami, you've been close to Key West. And if you've been to Key West, you've been close to Cuba, a long thin island in the Caribbean Sea. There is even a sign with an arrow in Key West that says "90 Miles to Cuba."

Most people speak Spanish in Cuba. But, just like in the United States, there are also many people who speak other languages including English and Chinese. But mostly they speak Spanish.

The capital of Cuba is Havana, and that is where my father was born. When he was young, my father did what many children do in Cuba: he went to the beach with his family. Cuba is an amazingly beautiful tropical island, and many of the people who live there live close to the water. He swam every day that he could. One day, a friend of his brought over some goggles so that they could both see under the water. My father had never worn goggles before. When he put the goggles on and put his head under the water, he saw it teeming with fish. My father and his friend both swam farther and farther out from shore, the fish getting more and more colorful and more and more beautiful.

As they swam, my dad saw in the distance a very odd-looking fish that swam quite quickly toward him. The closer it got, the bigger it got. The bigger it got, the bigger my dad's eyes got under the goggles. The fish was shaped like a torpedo, long and thin and muscular looking. It knifed toward my dad, chasing all of the other fish in its path. Its mouth was square and massive, its teeth long and sharp, almost canine in appearance. As it brushed past my dad, he saw the silvery countenance, powerful tail, and bluish color. It was a barracuda.

My dad and his friend swam back to the shore as fast as they could, and my dad never put the goggles back on again. But the next day, there he was again, swimming in the same water.

His friend said, "But the barracuda is still out there!"

My dad said, "Like my grandmother used to say to me in Spanish, 'Ojos que no ven, corazón que no siente.' If your eyes can't see it, your heart won't feel it."

My dad also did what nearly every single boy did and still does in Cuba and other Caribbean islands like Puerto Rico and the Dominican Rebublic: he played baseball. Every single day of the year, children played baseball, except during hurricanes. During hurricanes, they played a game called "Let's pray that our roof won't be torn off and flung into the sea and we all drown." That game is not as fun as it seems.

My dad says one reason the Cubans and other Caribbeans are great at baseball is for the simple reason that they played so much, and because of this, they would often lose the baseballs. When they did, until they could get another one, they would play with a bottle cork wrapped in electrical tape. They didn't always have bats, so they would use broom sticks. He said that if you can hit a tiny cork wrapped in black tape with a broomstick, hitting a large white baseball with a real bat is easy.

My dad dreamed of playing professional baseball, but as he got older, he also dreamed about becoming a doctor. He loved the complexities of the human body almost as much as the intricacies of deciphering a pitcher's curveball. One game, after ripping a three-run home run to center field, stealing a base, and turning a fierce double play, he realized that he wasn't even the best player on his team. If he worked very hard and had a lot of luck, he might make the pros, and then what? How long would he play? While if he went on to be a doctor, how many lives could he make better? How much more challenging and exciting would it be to pursue medicine? Besides, his mother told him not to be a *payaso*, a clown, but to be somebody. Be Dr. Sacre. He loved the ring of that. Dr. Sacre. While he still played a lot of baseball and to this day still has a powerful throwing arm, he soon dedicated all of his free time to his studies.

He was almost finished with medical school and about to fulfill his dream to be a doctor when the Cuban Revolution happened.

★ ★ ★ ★

In the 1950s, while my dad was happily playing baseball and unhappily swimming with the barracudas, the president of Cuba was a man named Fulgencio Batista. He was a bad man, a dictator, and he ruined that tropical paradise. In the United States, if an elected official is abusing his office or not taking care of the country, he or she will most likely be voted out in the next election. But in Cuba, there was no way to vote Batista out of office. Worse, if you spoke against him, he would have you sent to jail and sometimes even killed.

One of the people speaking out against Batista was an incredibly charismatic man named Fidel Castro. He had a vision for the country that would save it from the clutches of Batista, and many of the people supported his vision. After a three-year revolution against Batista, Castro and his armed supporters drove him out of Cuba.

Some people were very excited in Cuba, and the worst of Batista's abuses were eliminated, most notably the notorious relationship he cultivated with American organized crime. However, after taking power, Castro revealed that what he really believed in was a Communist government. In theory, Communism is a way to make sure that everyone is treated fairly. In practice, if often means denying some basic human rights, including the freedom of speech, the freedom of religion, and the freedom to vote for opposing candidates. It wasn't long until Castro began to seize people's homes and businesses and throw people in jail and sometimes worse if they didn't support his Communist revolution. It seemed to many Cubans they had forgotten the old saying, *más vale el malo concido, que bueno por conocer*; it's better the devil you know than the one you don't.

Some people were happy with what Castro did, but many people weren't. Those who weren't happy saw no easy way to get rid of him, and many of those who tried ended up in great trouble. Many of them left the island and fled to other parts of the world, with the majority landing in the United States, and many in Miami, to the neighborhood of Little Havana.

My dad and his family left and settled in Little Havana in Miami in 1960. They hoped that the change was temporary, and they dreamed of quickly returning to Cuba to resume their old lives. Every day those first few years after the revolution, as an exile in a foreign land, my dad dreamt of one day returning to Cuba to continue his practice as a doctor. He dreamt of it every time he showed up to work as a dishwasher at one of the fancy hotels in downtown Miami. But when it soon became clear that Castro wasn't going anywhere, he thought about becoming a doctor in the United States. When he mentioned it to his best friend, also a doctor in Cuba and a dishwasher at the same hotel, his friend told him the joke Miami Cubans tell each other whenever someone would talk about the old days: "A Great Dane and a little Chihuahua are talking on Calle Ocho in Miami. The Great Dane says, 'In Cuba, I had the best dog house, steaks for dinner, and the most beautiful girlfriends.' The Chihuahua looks up at the Great Dane and says, 'Yeah, well in Cuba, I was a Great Dane too.'"

Even some of his own family told him he was crazy, telling him there was no way he was going to learn enough English to pass the United States Medical Licensing Examination, and he would never be a doctor. But his mother told him there was nothing he couldn't do and that he was meant to be a doctor. With her support and tenacity, and after a long, hard struggle to learn English, he finally passed the exam and became a doctor in the United States.

His first real job as a doctor was in a hospital in Boston. At that hospital, he met and fell in love with a woman whose family also had fled a country that they loved. Her family had to leave Ireland, another beautiful island country, after the Great Irish Famine in the mid-1800s. After many years of hardships as immigrants in the

United States, her family had settled in Boston and began to thrive.

That Cuban man and that Irish-American woman got married, and nine months and one day later, I was born. I grew up speaking Spanish with my dad and English with my mom. I am a Cuban-Irish-American, born in Boston. I feel not wholly American and not fully Cuban or Irish, but somewhere in between. Growing up with a mix of cultures was often hard, as I often felt alone. There were very few others like me in the places I lived, and I felt like such an outsider. I didn't quite look like my cousins in Boston or my cousins in Miami, and I for sure didn't look like any of the kids in my neighborhood. Now that I am older, I realize what a blessing it was. I have three powerful, amazing cultures that have formed me: the Irish, American, and Cuban, each with a unique feature that informed whom I would become. The love of story from my Irish family, the tenacity of the American spirit, and the passion and love of laughter from my Cuban family all form the core of my life and work today. We moved around a lot when I was young and eventually settled in Delaware. Nearly every major school vacation, including summer vacation as I was growing up, I would spend time in Boston with my Irish family or in Miami with my Cuban family.

In my early adolescence, I mostly wanted to spend time in Boston. But by the time I got to high school, I reconnected with the Cuban side of my family. I would visit my grandmother Mimi at her house in the Cuban neighborhood of Little Havana in Miami, Florida. She lived with her two sisters in a small neighborhood called Aguadulce, Sweetwater, near the famous Calle Ocho (8th Street). Her house was connected to my uncle and aunt's house, where they lived with their daughter and granddaughter. Cuban families often live very close to each other, sometimes with three or four generations in the same house.

Every morning, Mimi would come into my room at what felt to me like the crack of dawn . . . 9:00 a.m. She'd pull the sheets off of me, tug at my big toe, sit me up, prop the pillow behind my back, and give me a glass of *café con leche*, a glass of sweetened hot milk with a touch of strong, black Cuban coffee. I'd eat a small breakfast of toast and cereal while she disappeared into the kitchen with her two sisters.

I loved the sounds of those three women cooking in the kitchen: chopping, talking, laughing, yelling, and the little sound of the pressure cooker tic-tic-ticking away as the smells of black beans, garlic, fried plantains (like bananas), and *ropa vieja* (which literally translates as *old clothes*, a delicious dish of shredded meat and tomatoes) filled the house.

At about noon every day, the whole family would gather at her table: my aunt and uncle and cousins from next door, my other uncle and his family from down the street, and often some of the neighbors. It was a huge feast every day.

I asked her once why they always ate at noon, and she said that's the way they did it in Cuba. I asked, "Why did they do it that way in Cuba?" She said that it got so hot in the middle of the day in Cuba that everybody would go home from the stores, business, and schools and shut them all down for about two hours. A typical school and work day in Cuba was from 8:00 a.m. to 12:00 noon, with a two-hour lunch break or *siesta*, and then back to school or work from 3:00 to 6:00 p.m. She said that because Miami was as hot as Cuba, they did the same here.

It would be a huge meal, so big that afterwards, nobody could do anything except slink over to the couch, plop down, and talk. More people would visit, and everyone would tell stories, laugh, gossip, discuss politics, and joke until the hottest part of the day was over and they all returned to work, school, or cleaning up after the meal.

In that living room, after eating, sitting on her white faux-leather couches, often crammed right next to my relatives, I heard many different family stories from my grandmother. Then, my favorite Cuban Uncle Tito would start with his jokes, often by saying, "Acabo de venir de Cuba," I just came home from Cuba . . . we knew this was a lie, because it was illegal to go to Cuba without special permission, and while it's a bit easier to go now, it's still very difficult.

He'd say, "I just came back from Cuba!"

Everyone would lean forward. "What's it like in Cuba now?"

"Oh, it's sad! Communism has ruined our home. There are lines for everything in Cuba. You have to wait in a line that is three blocks long for bread, five blocks long for sugar, and eight blocks long for meat. Yesterday, I was waiting in the meat line when a young boy came up behind me and said, 'You know what? I'm going to find Castro and I'm going to get rid of him, one way or the other!' He left. I waited, one hour, two hours, three hours, and the boy came back. I said, 'Did you get rid of Castro?' They boy said, 'You think this line is long, you should see that one!'"

The whole family would laugh, no matter how many times we heard it. He had a way of making the joke new every single time.

In the quieter moments, when the family was gone and the dishes put away, right before I would go outside to play with my cousin and friends down the street, I would ask my grandmother why they would joke so much.

She said they joke so much because it feels better to laugh than cry. She said, "If we spend too much time thinking about Cuba and thinking about all we lost and all we miss, nobody would want to get together and celebrate the fact that we are all alive, and together, and healthy." But then she would sigh and say, "No hay mal que por bien no venga!" This is an old Cuban *dicho*, or proverb, that means "there is nothing so bad that something good doesn't come from it." She told me if Castro didn't take over Cuba, my dad wouldn't have left and he wouldn't have met my mom and I wouldn't be here. She would tell me that she loves me so much that it was worth losing a tropical paradise for tugging me out of bed in the morning.

Then she would shove me out of the front door into the humid summer afternoon and tell me to not come home until it was dark: she had things to do.

I miss those moments in her living room, but I keep them alive in my talks with my dad and brothers and in the stories I tell and write. If one day I have to leave this country, I hope I have the same amount of strength and character to embrace the change while clinging to the family roots, stories, and meals together that made all of us so strong.

NAMES

uando mi papá vino de Cuba, no habló inglés, solamente español. Conocío a mi mamá, quien no habló español, solamente inglés. ¿Y sabes que pasó? Se casaron, y nací yo, hablando español con mi papá, y inglés con mi mamá. (When my father came over to America, he didn't speak a word of English. He only spoke Spanish. He met a woman who didn't speak a word of Spanish. She only spoke English. Do you know what happened? They got married, and they had me. I grew up speaking *español con mi papá* and English with my mom.)

In my Cuban family, we all have funny nicknames. My father's name is Antonio, like mine, but no one confuses us because everybody calls him by his nickname, "Ñico." My uncle's name is Raymundo, but his nickname is "Tito." My brother's name is Roberto, but his nickname growing up was "Pintico" because when he was born, my grandmother picked him up, and she said, "Ay, que pintico." I asked my dad what "pintico" meant because I couldn't find it in the dictionary. He said that "pintico" means "what a little cutie pie."

My brother Roberto hated being called "cutie pie," and I called him that all of my life, partly because I knew it aggravated him, but mostly because it so perfectly encapsulated who he was. He still is the cutest one in the family, and I am a little jealous of that. Okay, a lot jealous. When he was in eighth grade, I was in tenth grade and around fifteen years old. He had his first date with a girl named Michelle. When she came to our house, she had a nice, pretty dress on, and my brother looked very handsome. He tugged at his sleeves, and she looked at one small spot on the carpet, moving her foot back and forth over it.

I said, "Michelle, if you don't know what to say to my brother, you can talk to him about his nickname 'Pintico' or 'Cutie Pie.'" I pinched his cheek like my grandmother used to do, and my brother turned red, while she looked up from the carpet and giggled. It broke the ice, but my brother stayed mad at me for a long time.

My grandmother Mimi gave me my nickname. My name is Antonio, like my dad, so she called me "Papito," a name typically given to first-born Cuban males. It loosely translates as "little boy" or "little man." I loved my nickname and the way that my grandmother said it: "Papito. Papito. Papito!"

Most of the Cubans I know have multiple nicknames, and I have a whole bunch of them too, given to me mostly by members of my family. Which one is my favorite? I'd have to say, "Cool."

MY NAME IS COOL

When I was five years old, the night before my first day of school, I was excited and nervous. I was excited because my parents told me school would be so much fun. I was nervous because, well, it may seem kind of silly, but it was true: I had so many names, I had no idea what my real name was. I thought of how I got all my names.

When I was born, my mom called me Señor Magoo, or Mr. Magoo, from a cartoon character she used to love as a girl, because my eyes were so big, just like his. So I thought my name was Señor Magoo. When my uncle came to the hospital, he shortened it and just called me El Goo. So for a short time, my name was Señor Magoo, El Goo.

My papá and mamá couldn't put Señor Magoo, El Goo, on my birth certificate, so they called me Antonio Bernardo Sacre.

Antonio because my dad's name is Antonio. Bernardo because that was the name of my mom and dad's best friend at the time. Sacre because that is my dad's last name, and if we lived in Cuba, I'd get my mom's last name too. Babies in Cuba get both their dad's last name and their mom's last name. I was born in the United States, and even though I didn't have two last names like my dad, I liked all the rest of my names very much.

So then my name became Señor Antonio Bernardo Magoo Sacre, El Goo.

By the time they got me home from the hospital, my grandmother was waiting for us. She grabbed me in her arms and called me "Papito," a name many Cuban grandmothers call their *nietos* or grandsons.

So my name became Señor Antonio Bernardo Magoo Sacre, Papito, El Goo.

My older cousin hugged and squeezed me when she saw me for the first time. She really liked hugging and squeezing me. I didn't like the hugging so much, but I really liked my older cousin. I have no idea what her name is, either, because she has more names than I do. She called me "Coquito" or little coconut head because even though my eyes were so big, my head was so tiny.

My name kept growing! Señor Antonio Bernardo Magoo Sacre, Papito-Coquito, El Goo.

By the time I could walk, I walked fast—really fast. So fast, my parents and grandmother and big cousin and uncle could barely keep up with me. I could get to the glass elephants on the small table and the basket of marbles way over on the other counter at almost the same time, and sometimes they could catch me before I pulled them all to the ground. But not every time!

Because I walked so fast, I bumped into lots and lots of things. I always had tiny cuts and bruises on my head and arms. When my next-door neighbor Miguel saw me, he called me "Futinquito," or old, run-down jalopy. Since I pretty much always had tiny cuts and bruises on my head and arms, he pretty much always called me that.

"¡Aqui viene el Futinquito!" (Here's comes the jalopy!)

So my mom called me Señor Magoo, my Uncle called me El Goo, my birth certificate said Antonio Bernardo Sacre, my grandmother called me Papito, my cousin called me Coquito, and Miguel my neighbor called me Futinquito.

So I guess my name was Señor Antonio Bernardo Magoo Sacre, Papito Futinguito Coquito, El Goo.

The summer before my first year of kindergarten, I didn't want to go to school. Mi papá made up a great game to help me want to go. We made a boat out of cushions and pillows, a sail made from one of Mamá's old dresses, and hats out of newspaper. With these makeshift goods, we went on a sailing adventure. He was *el Comandante*, the commander, and I was *el Capitán*, the captain.

We sailed all around the world in our house and ended up on a small island in my dad's office that was full of books. I tried to read them, but I couldn't understand the words. My dad did. He's smart. I asked how he got so smart. He said that after a few years in school, I would be able to read them, too. I told him that after our sailing trip, I couldn't wait to go to school!

On our way back from our imaginary trip, I saw a mosquito land on my dad's rear end. I smacked it, hard! My dad whooped. I showed him the squashed bug on my hand, and he laughed and called me, "El Capitán de los Mosquitos."

So my name became Señor Antonio Bernardo Magoo Sacre, Papito Futinguito Coquito, El Captián de los Mosquitos, El Goo.

The night before kindergarten, I wasn't sure which name I would use at school. I decided to just go to sleep and work it all out in the morning. My abuela always said, "Mañana, sabiduría: the morning is wiser than the evening."

Finally, I woke up on the first day of school. I felt better! I left my *Capitán's* hat in my room and I went to my cousin's room.

"Good-bye, Coquito!" she said.

I hugged my mom.

"Adios, Señor Magoo!"

I kissed my grandmother.

"Hasta luego, Papito!"

I shook hands with my uncle.

"Tu-tú, El Goo!"

I walked out the front door. Miguel waved, "Cuidado, Futinquito!"

I walked down the street with my dad. I got to the school. He said, "¡Adelante, Capitán de los Mosquitos! Keep going, Captain of the Mosquitos!"

I entered the big door and walked to the hallway. I was scared. A huge man walked up to me. He said, "What's the matter?"

I looked up at him, and I was so scared that I didn't just cry or scream, I howled. He smiled, took my hand, and gently led me to my classroom. I felt better.

I walked into my classroom. It was so pretty! There were pictures everywhere, with little desks and chairs, and kids dressed in their best clothes. A happy teacher smiled at me and pointed toward an open desk. I sat down.

"I'm Mrs. Green." *La Señora Verde*, I thought, giving her her very own Cuban nickname.

She called off the other names from a book she held at her desk.

"Mary Smith!"

A little girl said, "Here!"

"Darrell Washington!"

"Here!"

"John Wilson."

"Here!"

She kept calling names, and children kept saying, here. Then she said, "There's one name that no one answered to. Antonio Sacre?"

I looked around the classroom.

"Antonio Sacre?" She asked again. Who was she talking about? She looked at me.

"Honey, are you Antonio Sacre?"

I said, "I don't really think that is my name." The kids laughed.

"Sure, you do honey; you're a big boy now. Aren't you Antonio Sacre?"

"Well . . ."

"You must be because everyone else has been called off the list by now."

"Actually, I think my name is Señor Antonio Bernardo Magoo Sacre, Papito Futinguito Coquito, El Captián de los Mosquitos, El Goo."

The class started to giggle.

"Don't be silly, dear, what is your name?"

"I'm pretty sure my name is Señor Antonio Bernardo Magoo Sacre, Papito Futinguito Coquito, El Captán de los Mosquitos, El Goo."

The class started to laugh louder.

"Please, don't cause a fuss on the first day of school. Your name is Antonio Sacre."

"Actually, I think my name is more than that. It's . . ." And before I could explain to the class how Cubans have so many nicknames, and how my uncle calls me one thing, and my cousin another, and my parents another, one student in the back of the room said, "Hey, it's Goo-Goo!"

Another added, "No, it's goober!"

One said, "Potato!"

"He's the kid-with-the-super-silly-name. Can't he take anything seriously?" said another.

"Captain Disaster!" said another.

Everyone laughed. I laughed too, but I didn't like the nicknames they called me as much as I liked the nicknames my family called me.

The teacher finally quieted down the class. She looked at me sternly. "Please walk back down to the office, talk to the principal, and come back here with a normal name."

On the long walk down the hall, I realized my name now was Señor Antonio Bernardo Goo-goo-goober Magoo Sacre, Potato Papito Futinguito Coquito, El Capitán de Disaster y los Mosquitos, Kid-with-the-super-silly-name, can't I take anything seriously, El Goo.

I walked into the office. The really big man who helped me earlier sat in a cozy chair and pointed to a chair next to him for me to sit.

"I understand there has been a ruckus in Mrs. Green's room."

I told him all that happened and he started laughing. "You, my friend, have a powerful, funny, amazing name, one that you should be proud of. You go back to the classroom and tell them that *is* your name. And add this one, from me."

He leaned over the desk, and he whispered it into my ear.

I smiled.

I walked back to my kindergarten classroom and charged through the door.

"My name is Señor Antonio Bernardo Goo-goo goober Magoo Sacre, Potato Papito Futinguito Coquito, El Capitán de Disaster y los Mosquitos, Kid-with-the-super-silly-name, can't I take anything seriously, El Goo. And the principal said so, and he said I could add The-kid-who-is-not-afraid-to-say-who-he-is. And he said, 'do you know what that makes you?'"

"What?" asked the children, laughing from their seats.

I crossed my arms in front of me, stood taller, and said, "Cooooooooolllllll. But, if you want, you can just call me cool. Cool?"

La Señora Verde smiled and said, "Cool."

I really liked school.

Food Fight

*W*hen I was eight years old, I settled down with just the nickname my family still calls me to this day, Papito, although I still answer to all the other nicknames. That year we moved to a small town in Delaware. Before that, we lived in Boston and Kentucky and Tennessee and Maryland. My dad kept transferring to better and better hospitals. No matter where we went, we always seemed to be the only bilingual family, and Delaware was no different. Nobody spoke Spanish there. It seemed like I was the only one; it was quite possible at the time that we were the only Spanish-speaking family in Delaware. On my first day of school, I think it was third grade, I was so excited and nervous to be there that I forgot to speak English. I walked in there and said, "Hóla. ¿Cómo están toda la gente aquí? Yo me llamo Papito."

The kids looked at me and said, "What?"

I said, "Hóla. Me llamo Papito."

My teacher said, "Honey, nobody speaks Spanish here. We only speak English."

I said, "That's okay, I speak English too. Hello, everybody. My name is Papito."

One little kid in the back of the room stood up, and he said, "P-P-Papito? Sounds like Dorito!"

I said, "No, no, no, it's Papito."

He said, "No, no, no. It's Dorito!" He called me "Dorito" for the whole first day of school. The next day when I showed up at school he called me "Nacho Cheese Head" and "Burrito" and even "Potato."

I went home that day and I said, "Papá, ahora yo no me llamo Papito."

He said, "¿Cómo? Tú te llamas Antonio."

I said, "No. Ahora, no me llamo Papito. Ahora me llamo . . . (y pensé del nombre más americano) . . . ahora me llamo Tony." I said that I didn't want to be called Papito anymore. I wanted to be called "Tony" (what I thought was a more American-sounding name).

My dad said, "¿Tony? Okay."

The next day he dropped me off at school. He said, "Hasta luego, Papito . . . uh, Tony. Adiós."

I said, "Okay, Papá. Adiós!"

One of the kids on the playground heard my dad and me speaking in Spanish. He was a huge fifth grader. In third grade, the fifth graders looked six feet tall to me. He walked over to me and said, "Hey!"

I said, "Yeah?"

He said, "What was that you were speaking?"

I said, "Spanish."

He said, "Spanish? Sounds stupid. Are you stupid?"

I didn't know what to say. I looked up at him and I said, "Uhhhhh . . . " and he told the whole school that I was stupid.

I went home and said, "Papa, ahora yo no quiero hablar español." I said, "I don't want to talk Spanish ever again."

My dad said, "¿Cómo? Tú puedes hablar español y inglés, los dos son muy importantes." He said, "You can speak Spanish and English, both are very important."

I said, "No. Ahora, I'm only speaking English." From that moment on until well into high school, if my dad spoke to me in Spanish, I'd answer him back in English. After a while, if he spoke to me in Spanish, I pretended like I didn't understand him until he only talked to me in English.

When I turned nine years old, my mom and dad got divorced and my dad moved away and I had no one to practice Spanish with, but that didn't bother me. My mom spoke English. All of my friends spoke English. I was going to speak English just like everyone I knew. As I got older, I forgot all the Spanish I ever knew, and by the time I got into high school, I couldn't speak a word of it.

When my grandmother Mimi heard from my father that I wasn't speaking Spanish anymore, she made him send me down to live with her for one whole month of my summer vacation in Little Havana in Miami, Florida. When I walked into her house for the first time in quite a while, she looked at me said, "Oye, Papito! Fsfjsccoalks-fqoirehhlksajdhflkajhf!"

I looked at her and waved. I said, "Hi, Mimi."

She said, "Oye, Papito! Fllkjfeoirsdfnaldfvalkseirutiu!"

When she saw that I didn't understand a word she was saying, she got mad. She started yelling, and I could understand a few words. This is what it sounded like to me: "Papito, lsdkjfdalskjdfdlaskdjf español fkfdjgflkdfjgfs Cubano gjfkeoirutlkjflirutoisu gringo!"

Then she grabbed me by my ear, and pulled me into the kitchen. She opened up the refrigerator door, reached

in, and she took out a piece of *flan* (flan is a brown, cus-
tard-like dessert that's really delicious).

She said, "Papito. Esto es un pedazo de flan."

I looked at her and I said, "Hi, Mimi."

She said, "No, '¡hi, Mimi'! ¡Flan!" She walked up to me
and stuck that flan in my face.

I said, "¡Flan!"

She said, "Beri goo." She reached into the refrigerator.
She got out the gallon of milk.

She said, "Papito, este se llama un galón de leche."

I said, "What?"

She unscrewed the top, walked over to me—BLUB,
BLUB, BLUB. "¡Leche!"

I said, "¡Leche!"

She said, "Beri gooo!" She reached into the refrigerator. She got the butter.

She said, "Papito, este se llama mantequilla."

I said, "Mante . . . mante . . . "

She said, "¡Mantequilla!" and stuck that in my face, too.

I said, "¡Mantequilla!"

She said, "Beri goo!"

Then she reached into the refrigerator, and she got the
eggs and the lettuce and the mayonnaise and the ketchup.
Every time she brought out something, if I could say it in

Spanish, I could grab it from her and throw it at her. If I couldn't say it in Spanish, she would throw it at me. Soon we had a great, big food fight in the kitchen, with food going everywhere, and we were laughing.

Then she took me in the bedroom, and she threw the sheets and the pillow, and every time she hit me with the pillow, she'd say the word in Spanish, but I'd forget because I always got hit with it. To this day I don't know how to say "pillow" in Spanish.

Then she took me into the bathroom, and she threw the soap and the shampoo and the toilet paper too. The word for *soap* is *jabón,* and the word for *soup* is *sopa,* and I would mix the two up all the time. I'd say, "Mimi, I'm gonna take a bath. Please come and give me the *sopa.*" She'd go to the refrigerator and get the big pot of soup and walk into the bathroom and say, "Here you go, Papito." I know the difference between *soup* and *soap* now.

Then she sat me down in the living room, and she told me many versions of the same story. She told them to me all summer in Spanish until I could tell them back to her entirely in Spanish. Now I'm going to tell you one of the many versions of the story, in English with a little flavoring of Spanish, so you can get a taste of what that story sounded like when she told it.

The Country Mouse

here once was a *Guajiro ratón*, or a country mouse, who lived in a fertile valley near the mountains of Pinar del Río on the westernmost part of the island of Cuba. He was a good farmer, and he worked very hard.

While he loved farming, he had a dream.

He sang all day as he worked, "I've got a dream. I dream. I dream when the ground is hard and the sun's so hot."

"What's your dream, Guajiro Ratón?" his papá would ask.

"To one day go visit Havana, the capital of Cuba!"

"Ay, niño, Havana is one of the most beautiful cities in the world, but it is so far away and there is much work to be done here on the farm. But al quien madruga, Dios le ayuda. If you wake up early in the morning, God will help you."

"That's right, Papá. A Dios rogando y con el mazo dando. I'll pray to God and hope God helps me, but I'll also do the work."

Every day, Guajiro Mouse would work and sing, sing and work, "I've got a dream. I dream. I dream when the ground is hard and the sun's so hot!"

But every year, something happened to prevent the little mouse from going to the capital city. One year there was not enough rain. The next, there was too much. And the next year there was a hurricane!

But still, he worked and sang, and sang and worked. One year, the crops were in and Papá was provided for, so Guajiro Mouse told his papá he was going to make the journey to Havana.

"Little mouse," said Papá, "before you go, remember, en boca cerada no entran moscas; a closed mouth catches no flies."

"Okay, Papá."

"Y todo que brilla no es oro; all that glitters is not gold."

"Sí, Papá."

"And dime con quien andas, te digo quien eres. Tell me with whom you walk, and I'll tell you who you are."

"Okay, Papá. I've heard these dichos, these sayings, many, many times."

"And one more thing. I love you."

"Y yo, Papá."

He promised to be back before the spring planting season, and after a great party with all of the village, he left.

He walked and he walked, and he walked and he walked, and finally got to the big city of Havana.

It was so beautiful! He saw the beaches, he saw the cobblestone streets, and he saw the cathedral. In the setting sun, it looked golden. He remembered his papá's words, not everything that shines is gold, but it sure looks pretty. He saw the spire and thought, if he could just get to the top of the spire, he would have a view of the whole city, and if he saw the whole city, what a tale he could tell back home! But he couldn't find a way up to the top of the spire no matter how hard he tried. He was disappointed, but the cathedral was so beautiful, and the spire so high, and every time he looked up at it, his mouth dropped open. He looked at it many times.

Then, he heard someone close by say, "En boca cerrada, no entran moscas! In a closed mouth, flies can't enter!" Guajiro Mouse laughed, and turned to see a Havana city mouse who was just his size, and just his age, but wearing the coolest hat he had ever seen.

"My dad told me that before I left Pinar del Río!"

"You live in Pinar de Río! I've always wanted to go there. What's it like?" asked City Mouse.

"Well, it is beautiful. We have rolling hills, and beautiful farms, and we are not far from the sea. But it's nothing really exciting. It's kind of boring, actually. Every day, I wake up, walk out to the fields, and work and sing, and sing and work, and every night we sit around and listen to the old people tell the same old stories."

"Ooh, I would love to see the fields, and watch you work and sing, and to listen to some of those stories!"

"Oh, if you came to visit, you would have to work, and the stories are lovely. What's it like here?"

"The same thing: the dancing, the singing, the eating, the parties, the corre-corre, the hustle and bustle. It's exhausting!"

"Ooh, that sounds great to me!" sighed Guajiro Mouse.

"I've got a great idea, why don't I show you around Havana, and then you can show me around Pinar del Río?"

"¡Fantástico! But I don't think I'm dressed well enough. My hat is not as nice as yours!"

Havana Mouse looked at Guajiro's hat.

"Well, it's true, my hat . . . is a haaattt, and your hat is a hat, but a hat is a hat, and that's that. Besides, two heads are better than one. Let's go!"

They walked past the cathedral, past the huge spire up on the top of the oldest cathedral in Old Havana.

Guajiro Mouse said, "I wish I could walk to the top of the spire and see the whole city, but I don't think there is a way up there."

"I know how to get all the way to the top of the spire!"

"How did you learn that?"

"Well, I went to the library, and I got all the books on the cathedral I could find, and I studied and studied and studied. And studied and studied and studied. And then I asked the mouse at the front door. Let's go!"

When they got to the top, and saw how beautiful the city looked, both of their mouths opened wide, even though they knew the old saying.

Havana Mouse said, "I haven't been up here in a long time. Sometimes, it takes someone from another place to make you appreciate what you have."

Havana Mouse showed Guajiro Mouse all around Old Havana, and the river, and the waterfront, and they finally made it to the famous Cabaret Nacional, where some of Cuba's best singers and musicians have played some of Cuba's most famous music for years.

"I'd love to go inside, do you know how we can get in?"

"I do!"

"How did you learn?"

"I studied and studied and studied, and then went to the box office, and I bought a ticket!"

They had a lovely time. When they left the Cabaret, they talked and they talked and they talked and they talked. The talked so much, they didn't really pay attention to where they were going, and soon found themselves in a dark alley.

"Oh oh, I goofed. We better turn around, quick, I think we are pretty close to the where the cat—"

"MEEOW!" A cat leapt down from a fence and blocked the only way out of the alley.

"Havana Mouse, what are we going to do?"

"My books didn't tell me what to do in this situation! But two heads are better than one, and mine's a blank right now, so start thinking!" Havana Mouse jumped and hid behind Guajiro Mouse.

The cat got closer and closer. Its claws extended, its eyes got smaller, and just as it was about to pounce,

Guarijo Mouse said at the top of his voice, "Bow wow wow wow wow wow!"

The cat stopped and stared at the two mice. He thought, "Wow, that mouse in back has one cool haaattt, and the mouse in front has just a hat, but the hat doesn't make the mouse, and two mice will taste better than one." He stepped closer.

Country Mouse barked even louder.

The cat stopped. He thought, maybe Country Mouse was calling the neighborhood dogs, and sure enough, in the distance, the dogs answered. County Mouse barked louder and louder. The dogs got closer and closer.

The cat got scared and ran away.

Havana Mouse said, "Wow, that was cool!"

Guajiro Mouse said, "Like my father always says, it's good to know another language!"

Havana Mouse said, "Wow! How did you learn to speak dog?"

And Guajiro Mouse said, "When I was younger, I went to my local library, and I studied and studied and studied, and . . . our next door neighbor was a Chihuahua. I called him Chi-wowwww wowwww wow wow wow."

"What did you say in dog to the cat?"

"I told him I had a black belt in Judo and that you were a black belt in Karate, hi-ya!"

Well, Havana Mouse learned to speak dog from Guajiro Mouse, and Guajiro Mouse learned all the songs and dances of old Havana. The Guajiro Mouse and the Havana Mouse had many more adventures in Havana and then set out to Pinar del Río, where they had many more adventures still. And you know this story is true, because if you go to the streets of Havana in the Fall, you can see at the top of the cathedral two little mice, one with a haaat, and the other with a hat, or if you go to the fields of Pinar del Río in the spring, you can see them working and singing, singing and working. *Colorín, colorado, este cuento se ha acabado*, a Cuban way of saying "the end."

I didn't know it at the time, but by telling me this and many other stories, my grandmother gave me the gift of my language again, a gift that I almost threw away as a teenager. Because of that gift, I eventually became a storyteller.

LEPRECHAUN'S GOLD

Created by Rives Collins and retold by Me

They say that if you find a leprechaun, grab on to him and don't let go of him. Now, he's going to run fast. You've got to stay with him. He's going to run under bushes. You've got to stay with him. He's going to try to trick you. He'll say, "Look over there!"

If you say, "What?" and let go of him for one second, he'll disappear. But if you're fast enough and clever enough and strong enough to hold on to him, he'll take you all the way to the very center of the woods, where you'll see the pot of gold and that rainbow. Also, you'll see next to it, on this little old wooden stump, a dirty gold coin. When you are there, you can let go of the leprechaun. The leprechaun will say, "Choose. You can choose whatever you want." Now, if you know this story, you won't choose that pot of gold because as soon as you put your hands in to scoop up all that gold, the pot of gold disappears, the rainbow disappears, the leprechaun disappears, and there you are, stuck, lost in the woods. But if you choose that little gold coin, the leprechaun will get so mad. He'll say, "No! Choose the pot of gold!"

You'll say, "Uh-uh."

"Choose the pot of gold!"

"Uh-uh."

"Choose the pot of gold!"

He turns bright red and he disappears in a puff of smoke, the rainbow disappears, the pot of gold disappears, you're still lost in the woods, but you've got this little gold coin. It's a magic coin. If you put it in your pocket and you find your way out of the woods, whenever you want to spend it, it's always there. You want to buy an ice cream? There it is. The next day you want to buy a hot dog? There it is. You want to buy some clothes? Just put your hand in your pocket. The coin is always there. It magically replicates itself in your pocket whenever you need to spend it . . . with one catch. You have to give that coin away to every single person you see.

If you were in a group of people, you couldn't speak or do anything until you had given that magic coin to every single person in that group. Each time you gave it away, another coin appeared in your pocket, and you always had it to spend. However, if you decided to skip somebody because you didn't like the way he or she looked, or you were having a fight with that person, or you thought that person would not spend it wisely, the coin would turn to dust in your pocket. The paradox is as long as you give it away, you'll always have it with you.

The Irish say the same thing is true about stories. If you don't pass them along, they turn to dust in your head and then they are gone.

WATER TORTURE

O n my very first birthday, the day that I turned one, my mom was in the hospital giving birth to twin boys. She came home carrying two ugly, stinky, bald, disgusting baby boys. My mom said she put them in the crib and I was so mad I looked up at her and I stood on her toe.

My mom says that twins can communicate with each other, even in the womb, and my brothers were no exception. When they were in their crib, they would speak baby talk to each other, and I would stand over their crib and get angry because Henry, the oldest, would look at the younger and say, "Aysabaysabaysabaysabuhbuhbuh?"

Robert, the younger twin, would answer him back, "Aysabaysabaysabuhbuhbuh," and the two would have a conversation for hours. I was so jealous that they could understand each other and that I had no idea what they said.

I'd say, "Mom, what are they saying?"

She'd say, "They're talking baby talk, Hon."

Oh, I'd get so mad. And they knew it, because after a while they'd look up at me and say, "Aysabaysabaysabuh?" And both would point at me, "Hee hee hee hee hee!" I'd get so mad, I'd poke at them through the crib bars.

When they got out of the crib, that's when the trouble began because there were two of them and one of me and they went after my toys. I remember one day my brother Robbie, the younger twin, grabbed my favorite toy—my fire truck. Uncle Tom was a fireman, and he gave me that truck. You could pull the ladder out, open the little door, and push the little horn. When Robbie took it, I got so mad that I chased him all around the house and trapped him in a corner. I looked down at him.

I said, "Gimme back my fire truck."

He looked up at me and said, "Uh-uh."

I said, "Gimme back my fire truck."

He said, "No way."

I said, "Gimme back my fire truck . . ."

He had nowhere to run. He looked all around. All of a sudden he pulled open his diaper and stuck the fire truck right in his diaper. Oh, I was so mad I reached forward and ripped his diaper right off. He started to cry. Henry, his twin, connected at some level and started to cry too. He pulled *his* diaper right off. Then the two started to laugh. They both went running out the door and ran down the street naked as can be, just as my mom was coming home. You know who got in trouble? I did.

My brothers and I fought all the time, but the day we fought the worst was September 23rd, our birthday. If my mom bought us all different gifts, we would run after each other to get each other's gift, and then we'd break it, until we all had broken all of the gifts. So my mom figured out she had to buy the exact same gift for all three of us.

Not only that—we had to open it up at the exact same time. If I got a shirt, they got a shirt (different size). If I got a toy, they got a toy (different color). Also, she began to make three birthday cakes for us, and we were allowed to invite five friends from school—no more, no less. All the neighborhood kids were invited and then all of our cousins (we didn't have to waste an invitation on them). So we would have fifty kids, most of them boys, running around the neighborhood on September 23rd. My mom said it never rained on September 23rd, and to this day, wherever my mother is, it doesn't rain on that day.

I remember the year that I turned ten years old (my brothers were turning nine). I got special privileges that year. My privilege was that I got to stay up one whole hour later than my brothers. I used that hour wisely. I watched TV. Lots of it.

The night before my birthday, I stayed up and watched this old black-and-white World War II movie. In it were armies, tanks, planes, and all kinds of things that I thought were really cool. And then there was this spy. But this was a *real spy*—not like James Bond, who I still thought was really cool. This spy went in and out of places, got secrets, sold secrets. I was so excited about that spy when all of a sudden the spy got caught, and he got tortured.

They strapped him to a metal table, they pulled a water faucet over his head, and they scientifically calibrated it so one drop of water would drop from that faucet every sixty seconds right between his eyes. They had strapped his head and his arms down so that he couldn't turn away.

Now you may not think that's such a bad torture, and the spy didn't either.

He said, "I'm not telling you anything." But after one hour of water torture, after two hours, three hours—not being able to drink the water, not being able to go to sleep because every time he did the drop would wake him up, and not being able to turn his head—he began to shake.

After twelve hours, the spy was giving up everything he knew.

The next day was my birthday. *Their* birthday. September 23rd. It was a really hot day that fall, so my mom decided that instead of all the games we usually played (which we loved to play) like tag, catch, and Red Rover, Red Rover (where you join hands and say, "Send Robbie right over"), that day we were going to have a water balloon fight.

It was excellent. My mom went to the hardware store, she bought a big bag of 500 multi-colored balloons, and the three of us didn't fight that morning as we filled up those water balloons. We filled up balloon after balloon, and when our friends came, we spread the balloons out all over the neighborhood—under cars, next to bushes, on the steps—all over the place.

Then the water balloon fight began. But it wasn't a water balloon *fight*. It was a water balloon WAR! It was epic. There were balloons everywhere. Kids were getting drenched. Adults were getting drenched. Dogs and cats were getting drenched. It was great!

In the middle of all that mayhem, I decided it was time for me to catch a spy. I tried to catch my friends. They were too fast. I tried to catch my brother Henry. He was too big. I caught my brother Robbie, the younger twin, and threw him on the ground. I put my knees on his elbows and spread his arms against the ground. I used to do that when I tickled him under the arms, but this time I got one of those water balloons, I untied the little knot, I held it high above my head, aimed it right between his eyes and said, "Robbie, time for . . . *water torture.*" BLOOP. Right between the eyes. BLOOP. Right between the eyes.

Robbie looked up at me with his big brown eyes and said, "Tony, I would really appreciate it if you would stop doing water torture on my head."

"Time for more *water torture!*" BLOOP.

At this point my friends were nearby. They had seen the show and they were laughing. They knew what I was doing. My brother looked up at me.

He said, "No, Tony. Really. Mom always says whenever you aggravated me to ask you politely to stop. Well, this is aggravating. Would you please stop?"

"Time for more *WATER TORTURE!*" BLOOP.

At this point my brother's face turned bright red. I could see the water begin to bead on his forehead. The veins popped out of his wrists. He said, "Tony, I'm asking you politely to please stop doing water torture on my—" BLOOP.

At this point, Robbie's arms were shaking so much. Then my life, in my memory at least, went into slow motion. With a strength I did not know he had, he shoved upward with his arms, flinging me into the air, and I found myself flying backwards away from him. I landed on my back in the middle of the street.

"Ow!"

My friends were laughing. Robbie got up and ran in slow motion around the back of the house. Balloons were going everywhere. Then my life returned to normal motion—laughter, balloons going everywhere. Then Robbie came back from around the house (slow motion again), hands gripping a segment of the backyard fence that he ripped off. I could see the nails glinting in the sun, dirt hanging from the other end. I said, "Maaaa . . ."

I went running inside, slammed the door, and went to the safest place I could think of—the bathroom—and locked it. Then I waited. I heard the front door open and slam shut. The little doorknob on the bathroom door started to jiggle. I said, "MAAA . . . "

BOOM! BOOM! BOOM! He smashed at the door. Then he got a bobby pin and began to pick at the lock. Mom didn't like that we knew how to do that. The door opened. There he stood, hands gripping that wood, nails glinting in the light of the bathroom mirror. He swung that board as hard as he could, just missed my head, and smashed it into the bathroom mirror.

Glass went everywhere. My mom appeared out of nowhere. Thank goodness. She picked up Robbie with her hand, lifted him in the air (his feet were dangling—I didn't know my mom was that strong), and said, "Do you want to kill your brother?"

Robbie yelled, "Yes!"

My mom picked me up and brought us both into the kitchen, sat us down, and said, "Now, tell me what happened."

We both started talking at the same time.

"He tried to kill me with a board!"

"He did water torture on my head!"

My mom said, "Alright, now, listen. Let me see now. Tony, you did water torture on your brother's head. That was bad. Robbie, you tried to kill your brother with a board. That was bad. I want you both to apologize to one another."

"I'm not apologizing because he tried to kill me."

"I'm not apologizing because he did water torture first."

My mom said, "I don't care who apologizes first. Neither of you is getting any cake unless you each apologize."

Now, my mom's cake is the most incredible cake in the world. It's so big and the frosting is so thick. It's very delicious. We both looked at the cake, and Robbie looked up at my mom with those big brown eyes.

She said, "Don't you give me that look."

He looked at the cake. I knew that Robbie would crack first. I knew how much he loved that cake. I loved it too, but I was a whole year older. I wasn't going to crack. He looked at me.

He quickly said, "I'm sorry." He looked to my mother and said, "Can I have some cake, Ma?"

She said, "Not unless you *sincerely* apologize."

Out of the corner of my mouth I said, "Yeah. *Sincerely* apologize."

My brother said, "Awww." But he looked at that cake, looked back at my mom, then looked at me.

He said, "Tony, I wasn't really going to kill you with that board. I just wanted you to stop, but I went about it the wrong way, and I'm sorry I did that."

My mom smiled and said, "Very good, Robbie. You get a piece of cake."

Robbie said, "Aw thanks, Ma." She handed him a big piece of cake on a white paper plate, and just as he put that plastic fork into that amazing five-layer cake with all that frosting and brought that fork to his mouth, he looked at me and said, "Mmm mmm mmm. Your turn to apologize to me."

I got so mad I said, "Mom. Now he's making fun of me!"

My mom said, "Well, just apologize."

"I'm not going to apologize."

Robbie said, "You gonna apologize?"

He was moving that cake so close to my nose and eating it. I got even madder. I wasn't going to apologize.

He went outside and started to play. All the kids came in and got their cake. I sat there and sulked. Finally, that night, everyone was gone and it was just me and that cake and my mom.

My mom said, "Honey, when I was your age I got into a fight with my older brother, and we fought for so long we didn't talk for almost four years. Luckily, we got over it and are friends now, but it was such a waste. I don't want that to happen to you. I want you to be good friends with your brother. It's important." I thought *Yeah, Ma. Whatever*.

For the rest of our birthday, I didn't talk to my brother. And as one small thing can lead to a larger thing, the next day we didn't talk either. And as a large thing can lead to a huge thing, we didn't talk all week. I never apologized.

Time passed and my brother and I rarely talked. We spoke to each other the absolute minimum that we needed to coexist in the same house. "Gimme the salt!" and "Get out of my room!" Things like that.

Then I entered junior high school and I had other friends. Then I went high school and . . . who needed a little brother anyway?

When I turned sixteen, I passed my driver's education exam and I received my little, magical driver's license. I said, "Ma, can you buy me a car?"

She said, "Honey, you've got to work for a car. We don't have that kind of money."

I went to my father. He said, "I won't buy you a car either. You have to work for it."

So I did. I worked at the Lobster Shanty near my house. I cleaned dishes all summer long. I would come home smelling like fish, lobster, and crab. It was disgusting, but by the end of the summer I had saved $500, enough to buy a "beater" car.

I drove it home. I was so excited. I drove up to my house and beeped the horn. It didn't work. I tried to roll down the window; the handle came off in my hand. I finally opened the door and yelled, "Hey everybody, come out and see my new car!" They came out, and my mom was so happy for me. Even Robbie looked at it and seemed to be impressed.

The car was a mess, but I loved it. Every few weeks it would not start, and my brother Robbie would come out and fix it. He was always good at fixing the lawnmower, and he loved fixing my car. Even though we weren't friends, it was still nice that he was fixing my car. Then he began to teach me the things he was doing, and little by little, through that old beater car, my brother and I began to speak again. I still didn't apologize, but at least we were talking.

Then my father paid for a new paint job, upholstery, tires, and brakes. He spent almost two thousand dollars fixing up the car. I asked why he was doing that now. He said, "I want my son to drive a safe car, so that's why I got the tires and brakes, and I want my son to look good in his car, and that's why I painted it."

I said, "But you could have helped me buy the car in the first place."

He said, "I wanted to make sure you were willing to work hard for something before I helped you. That's how I got to where I am now."

As time passed, my brother turned sixteen and got his license, and he said, "Tony, we've been friends now for a while, haven't we?"

I said, "Yeah, Robbie. We have."

He said, "Well, do you think we're best friends?"

I said, "No, we're not best friends, but we're pretty good friends."

He said, "Well, Good Friend, older brother of mine, can I borrow your car?"

I smiled, "Of course you can borrow my car."

And we shared it. He would take it to work or to the movies. I would take it to school. One day I was at my friend's house. When I came home, my mom was sitting in the kitchen. Usually she was in the living room, but this day she was in the kitchen.

I said, "Ma, what's up?"

She said, "Well, Honey. Robbie's okay. He's upstairs. He smashed the car. He's okay, though. He's worried you're going to kill him. Honey, don't kill him."

I was happy he was fine, but as I walked up the stairs, I thought of every single dish I had to clean to get that car. I thought of all the money my father put into painting and new tires. I thought about how now I had no way to get to school. I was so mad. I forgot that it was an accident, and as I opened up his door, I stormed into his room, but there he was, asleep on his little bed.

It looked like had been crying in his sleep, and on his forehead was a big, red bump. I sat on the bed and gently shook him awake. He looked up at me. He started crying again.

He said, "Tony, are you gonna kill me?"

I said, "Robbie, were you wearing a seatbelt?"

He pointed to his head. "No. How do you think I got this?"

I said, "Robbie, you weren't wearing a seatbelt. You smashed the car that I washed thousands of fishy dishes for. You know what that means?"

Robbie said, "What?"

I said, "It's time for . . . *WATER TORTURE.*"

Robbie started to laugh, and we a made a promise to each other to always wear a seatbelt after that. And even though I never did get another car as cool as the 1970 Dodge Dart Swinger, I do have a new best friend, and that's my little brother Robbie.

Frijoles and Fans

$\mathscr{M}$y grandmother, Mimi, would get up every morning at 5:30 and go straight to the kitchen and begin to cook, clean, iron, do the laundry, and have the whole place tidy and clean by 8:30 when her older sister, Nina, who was eighty-five-years-old at the time, would wake up. Now, Nina would get up very late by Cuban women's standards, and she would come to the kitchen, sit down at the table, and eat her piece of toast that Mimi had prepared hours before. She would chew it twenty times, like they taught her in Havana when she was very young. From all the effort expended from eating that piece of toast, she would have to go back to her room, lie down, and take a little nap. Mimi, the whole time, couldn't stand seeing her sister napping around like that. She'd go up into the bedroom and she'd say, "¡Nina! ¿Qué tu crees, que aquí no trabajabamos? ¡Levántate, Chica! ¡Levántate! Now get up and go to work!"

Nina would look up at Mimi and say, "Ay, Mimi. ¡Por Dios!" But Nina would get up and do the only task she could do, which was sort the beans. We'd eat beans every day in my grandmother's house, and they'd come in their natural state, with little stones in them that you'd have to pick out, and you'd have to wash the rest of the beans. It takes me about five minutes to sort a few pounds of beans. It takes Mimi about five seconds. Well, Nina would sit down with that great, big pile of beans, put her glasses on the edge of her nose, pick up one of those beans, hold it up to her glasses, look at it, and say, "Buen frijole. Good bean," and put it on the right. "Buen frijole. Good bean," and put it on the right. "¡Malo!" and throw it in the gar-bage. It would take her about four hours to do the whole stack of beans, just in time for dinner.

There are two things you need to know before you eat dinner with Cubans: the only way to prove that you like the food is by eating everything on your plate and asking for a second helping. If you don't eat two servings, and they are *full servings*—huge spoonfuls of rice and beans and meat and plátanos and avocado—you are insulting the cook. Don't eat three or they'll call you a pig. The second thing is you can't leave until the oldest person leaves from the table. So Nina was the oldest, and until she was finished chewing her two helpings, we couldn't leave. There were days it would take almost two hours. A lot of the time we didn't mind because Mimi would tell jokes and stories, but other times, we couldn't wait to get outside and play.

After eating, Mimi would clean the dishes away, and Nina wanted to teach me Spanish, just like Mimi had done my first trip there. She would hold up things on the table. She would say, "¡Papito! Este se llama una servilleta."

I would say, "¡Servilleta!"

She would say, "¡Muy bien!" She would go over a lot of the things on the table.

Now, my brother Henry never forgot his Spanish, so whenever Nina would give me Spanish lessons, he would often get upset. He would sit and shuffle in his chair, slap his head, look at his watch and drum the table, but he would not leave until Nina was finished. Well, after a few weeks of these Spanish lessons, Nina decided that for every word of Spanish she taught me, I would teach her the English equivalent.

She said, "¿Papito, cómo se dice *servilleta* en inglés?"

And I would say, "*Servilleta* quiere decir *napkin*."

She would say, "Nyai-ken," and I would say, "No, Nina. Nap-kin."

"Nyai-keen."

Well, Henry at this point had had it up to here. He grabbed the napkin from Nina. He said, "Nina, este no se llama *napkin*, este se llama *booby-booby*." Nina said, "Oo-hhh, booby-booby."

She picked up the knife. She said, "¿Cómo se llama este cosa en inglés?

Henry said, "Nina, esta se llama *butt-butt*."

Nina said, "Eh . . . butt-butt? Ohhhhh."

Soon everything on the table was named some variation of *booby-booby* or *butt-butt* or *butt-booby* or *booby booby butt butt* until Nina, who was not a silly woman, looked at the two of us. She said, "Oye, muchachos. Yo no creo que todas las cosas aquí en la mesa se llama *booby-booby* ni *butt-butt*."

We started to giggle. She said, "¡Ah-ha! Yo voy a llamar tu Tío Tito."

Our eyes got big. We said, "¡No! No llama a Tito."

She said, "Sí. Yo voy a llamarlo."

She picked up the phone. She dialed the numbers. She said, "Tito. Dicen los muchachos que todas las cosas aquí en la mesa se llaman *booby-booby* y *butt-butt*. ¿Qué cosa es *booby-booby* y *butt-butt*?"

Nina's eyes got big, her mouth opened, and she stared at the phone, then she carefully hung up the phone. As soon as that phone touched the cradle she said, "Tito viene!" and Tito appeared in the doorway and threw open the door. He was 6'2" and he used to be a boxer in pre-revolutionary Cuba. He came striding in and he said, "Oye. Dice Nina que toda las cosas en la mesa se llama *booby-booby* y *butt-butt*." He pointed at me. He said, "Tú es *booby-booby*," and he pointed at Henry and said, "Tú es *butt-butt*."

He picked up the napkin and said, "Papito. ¿Cómo se llama esta cosa en inglés?

I said, "Napkin."

He said, "Nyai-keen. Berri goo." He slammed it down.

He picked up the knife. He said, "Henry. Cómo se llama esta cosa en inglés?

Henry said, "¿Booby-booby?"

Tito's hair, which he had parted over his bald spot, started to tremble, and his face turned bright red. He picked up Henry with his thumb and forefinger. I started to giggle; he said, "You want a piece of this?" He picked me up, threw us both into the bedroom, shut the door, and *nos dio un tempeste tan grande*, which is like a Cuban hurricane. The whole neighborhood could hear it. When he brought us out, Henry looked like he was going to giggle again, but he held it in. Tito looked like he was just coming out of a boxing match. Nina was scared on the couch. She went to say something to Tito. He looked at her and said, "Nina, deja. Be quiet."

He looked at us. He said, "You two respect these women." He ran out of the house, jumped in the car, and spun his wheels out of there. As soon as that car hit the pavement, the phone started ringing. It was my Aunt Mary from way down the street. She heard the yelling and said, "Papito. ¿Cogiste un tempeste de Tito, verdad?" She hung up the phone.

My dad called from Delaware. He said, "Muchachos, I heard you got a little talking-to from Tito, huh? Dat's my boys!" He hung up the phone.

My mom called from Boston. She hadn't called that number in years, since the divorce. She said, "Hey, boys. Is everything okay down there? I'm getting some bad vibes up here!"

The next day, my family decided I should go to work at my Uncle Tito's factory. I started soon after that. I got up at 5:30 in the morning and took two buses to downtown Miami, near the Orange Bowl Stadium where the Miami Dolphins football team used to play.

On one side of the factory, the women sat hunched over their sewing machines, methodically piecing fabric together. On the other side, the men rolled out huge swaths of fabric on long tables, pinned patterns to the top, and cut the fabric with a large jigsaw. Another would cart piles of the fabric to the sewing women. In between the cutting men and the sewing women were two wizened, old women: the ironing women. Their job was to take the newly-stitched crumpled shirts, place them on an ironing board, pull down an industrial-size iron that hung on giant springs from the ceiling, and iron them into brand new steaming shirts, ready for market.

My job was to stand next to those women, take the new shirts, place them on a hanger, button all of the buttons, pull a transparent plastic bag over them, and load them onto a rack. As soon as the rack filled up, I would load the shirts on the truck for the afternoon deliveries. If I worked as fast as I could, I kept up with the two ironing women, clearing the shirts from their rack just as two more perfectly ironed shirts appeared in a cloud of steam.

Uncle Tito sat at his desk in the middle of the factory, surveying the workers, talking on the phone, and keeping the books. He always had a cup full of perfectly sharpened pencils on one corner of his spotless desk and a large cigar streaming blue smoke into the air on the other. Every now and then, he would take a puff of his cigar and look down at us. We all began to work even harder. Then he would go back to his books, and we would relax ever so slightly.

On my third day working there, I fell a shirt behind. The women were kind to me and they worked around my slowness. After an hour, I fell three shirts behind. While not missing a stroke of their iron, they whispered to me to try and catch up. I tried, but my fingers were cramping and the steam stung my eyes, and soon I was five shirts behind. They urged me along, pleading with me to catch up, all the while placing shirt after shirt on the rack. Now I could barely button one button, sweat ran down my back, a new shirt slipped from the rack to the factory floor, and the women were in a state of panic. I fell nearly thirty shirts behind. All of a sudden Tito slammed his pencil on the desk. It retorted over the loud factory din like a gunshot.

He strode over in three giant steps, looked at me, looked at the shirts, and whirled his fingers through the tangled mess of shirts, magically buttoning, bagging, and racking all thirty shirts in what seemed like thirty seconds. He pointed at me and said, "I talk to you at lunch." The women barely looked at me as we continued working.

At lunch, a little whistle blew. Usually, everybody ate their sandwiches and drank their coffee at their stations while Manolo would play salsa music on his old radio. On that day, however, everybody grabbed their lunch boxes and walked out of the factory into the Miami heat.

I walked over to Uncle Tito's desk and stood in front of it alone. He looked at me up and down, blew out a huge cloud of smoke, and said, "What's a matter with you? You are not a Sacre, because you do not work hard. I work hard, your grandmother work hard, your father work hard, but you are a piece of junk. You have the easiest job in the factory and you can't do it? You do not deserve the name of Sacre."

At this point I did the worst thing I could do as a Cuban male adolescent in my uncle's factory. I started to cry, and Tito, who had probably never seen a male cry before in his life, looked confused. He stammered, "What, what what what what, you feel bad? You feel bad? Well, I feel bad. I feel pain, but I don't cry!" He searched around his desk, grabbed the sharpest pencil he could find with his right hand, held out his left hand, and jabbed the pencil into his palm. It stuck there for a moment, and then he pulled it out. I could see the mark that the point made in his palm, a drop of blood rapidly forming. He looked startled and he yelled, "You see! That hurt me, but I don't cry! Now you work harder!"

I said, "OK, Uncle Tito!"

For the rest of the summer, I did. When I told Mimi about what happened at the factory, she rolled her eyes and said, "That's Tito."

WHAT YOU SAY

A s an adult, years later, I went back to visit Nina and Mimi one summer. I'd heard that Mimi was a little sick, and I wanted to see her. When I got there she was sitting on their back porch, where it was very hot. The doctors had told her to stay inside the house where it was air-conditioned, but she said, "No, no, no, no. Yo me voy a sentar aquí en mi silla."

She wanted to sit in her old rocking chair in front of the old, oscillating fan that looked like it was the only thing she had brought over from Cuba. Nina sat next to her, I sat in the middle of both of them, and the three of us just rocked. That fan would blow on Mimi and blow on me and blow on Nina and blow on me and blow on Mimi. We would sit and watch *telenovelas*, the old Spanish soap operas that Mimi and Nina watched for hours. They knew all the characters. They would raise their penciled-in eyebrows in mock horror at the twists and turns, yell at the screen, and make me promise I'd never, ever act like the *sin verguenzas* on the screen. There was no other place I'd rather be.

After a while, Mimi would look at me and say, "Papito. ¿Cómo van las cosas allí en Chicago? How are things going in Chicago?"

I told her how I was storytelling and acting and how I got knocked out in tae kwon do. Nina would laugh and Mimi would laugh too. Mimi said, "¿Diciendo cuentos, eh? Telling stories. Díme un cuento tú." She said, "You tell us a story."

I smiled, turned down the TV (Nina wouldn't let me turn it off), and told them the story that I had heard from a high school student in Chicago. He was from Guatemala, and this was a Guatemalan story that he told me that I told Mimi and Nina.

I said in Spanish, "Once upon a time there was a man named Miguel who lived in Guatemala, but his mamá was very sick, and he didn't have money to buy her medicine. He knew that if he got to America he would find someone who would give him money so he could buy medicine for his mamá. So he made the long, tough journey all the way through Central America and up through Mexico, and he finally crossed the border into the state of New Mexico, into a little town called Las Cruces.

"Now, at the time, nobody in Las Cruces spoke Spanish. They all spoke English, and Miguel knew no English. He walked around looking for the richest person in town. Finally, he stopped someone on the street and asked him the name of the richest person in town who could give him money to save his mamá, but he asked in Spanish and this is what it sounded like: 'Oye. ¿Cómo se llama la persona más rico en todo este pueblo quien puede darme medicina porque mi mamá esta muy enferma allí en Guatemala?'

"The person on the street looked at Miguel and said, 'What you say?'

"Miguel said, 'Oh. Gracias,' and he started to look around town for the man called 'Whatyousay.'

"He walked until he saw a huge house. It was a big mansion with a big gate in front of it, and he knew that Whatyousay probably lived in that house, but he had to be sure. So he asked a woman on the street. He said, 'Oye. ¿Quién vive en esta casa tan grande?'

"She looked at him and she said, 'What you say?'

"He said, 'Ay, gracias,' and he waited in front of that house.

Just then on the street behind him was a long row of black carriages. He looked at them, and in the back of that row was a huge box. *Una caja de muertos.* A coffin. Miguel walked down, tapped someone on the shoulder, and asked her who was in that box, but he asked in Spanish. He said, '¿Quién murió en esa caja de muertos?'

"She looked at Miguel and said, 'What you say?'

"Miguel said, '¡Ay, Dios mio! Whatyousay se murió.' He said, 'Oh my goodness! Whatyousay is dead!' He went back to Guatemala, and his mamá died."

Mimi and Nina started to laugh. They said, "Ay, que bueno." They loved the ending of that story. I told them that it was the way the boy told it to me.

They said, "¡Ay, Dios mio!" They laughed and talked about "Whatyousay," and then Nina told me to turn up the volume on the TV.

Mimi looked at me and she said, "Oye. Tienes que hablar las dos idiomas. You have to speak two languages."

I looked at Mimi. I said, "What you say?" She started to laugh.

She said, "Es verdad. You'd *better* know how to speak two languages!"

I studied English in college. Then I decided to be an actor, so I moved to Chicago. As an actor, I was told by my agents that I was "too ethnic" for most roles I would audition for, and "not ethnic enough" for the rest. I found myself in the place I find myself to this day, as the whitest person in some places and the least white in others.

I discovered a love of storytelling and began to study and practice the craft. My big break happened by accident, the day I became a bilingual storyteller. I was telling Davey Crockett, one of the only stories I knew. "Davey, Davey Crockett, king of the wild frontier!" As I was telling it, most of the children seemed enthralled with the story, but some of them weren't paying attention at all. Some instinct kicked in, and I started telling the story in Spanish. The children who weren't paying attention were suddenly delighted and amazed that somebody was speaking Spanish—their own language—from the stage, and they were loving it.

Then the English-speaking kids said, "What's he saying? Speak English!"

I switched back to English, but the Spanish-speaking kids said, "¡No, habla Español otra vez!"

So I switched back into Spanish, and before long I was saying things like, "Ven acá tu pesky varmint por que voy a shoot you!"

And all the kids were laughing and participating and translating for each other. After the assembly, the principal came rushing down with my check for fifty dollars, more than a whole shift at the coffee house. She said there were thousands of schools all over this country who needed someone like me. Almost overnight, I became a professional bilingual storyteller, which was difficult because I only knew a few stories.

The first stop for me was to my local library. Carolyn Prapocki, the children's librarian at the Logan Square Library in Chicago, directed me to the 398.2 folktale section, and I immersed myself in all the stories I could. I started with the Grimm tales and the Arabian nights, and moved through as many of the other fairy tales and folk stories I could find. She was instrumental to me in my early career. She shared with me that over a million people in Chicago had origins in Mexico or in Puerto Rico, so I studied as many of those stories as I could. My studies eventually led me to Mexico, where I spent countless days wandering the country, learning what I could about the culture, and discovering the diverse, fantastic, and often mystical stories that form part of the fabric of that beautiful country.

Just a short bus ride outside of Mexico City lies the ancient, mysterious city of Teotihuacan, where two of the largest pyramids in the Western hemisphere are situated, called the Pyramid of the Sun and the Pyramid of the Moon. They are connected by the Avenue of the Dead. Many times, I climbed the pyramid of the sun and surveyed the ancient city.

I would like to share with you a creation story from the Nautl people, the story of the sun and the moon, as well as other famous stories from Mexico, in the way I tell them.

The Rabbit in the Moon

*W*hen I was a child, my mother would ask me if I could see the man in the moon. I never could. When I was in Mexico, I learned that the people there see a rabbit in the moon, and there is a famous story as to why that is so.

Many ages ago, there was no sun and no moon, so the gods met in Teotihualcan to make the sun and the moon. They built a huge fire (*un gran fogón*), and they realized that somebody needed to jump in the fire and carry the hottest part of the fire into the sky, where it might become the sun. They asked, "Who will be brave, who will be the first to jump into the fire?" Nobody volunteered. The fire was too hot.

Finally, one of the gods stepped forward. His name was Tecuziztequetatl. Tecuziztequetatl was tall and handsome. He had an incredible headdress of feathers going off of his head, a green jade necklace, and a beautiful *tilma* (an incredible robe) tied with a gold and silver belt. He had around his ankles the ceremonial shells with stones in them, carefully strung together, that shook when he walked. He alone volunteered. He alone stepped forward. He glistened, incredible in that firelight.

When they said, "Well, who wants to be the moon?", nobody volunteered. If they were going to sacrifice themselves in the fire, they were going to be the sun, not the pale moon. Finally, a little voice said, "Yo quiero ser la luna."

The gods turned around. "That's great. Who said that?" They didn't see anybody.

"¡Yo, yo! I want to be the moon! ¡Yo quiero ser la luna!" They looked all around.

"¡Yo, aquí, aquí, aquí!"

They looked down to the ground, and there was tiny little Nanahuatzin. They said, "Nanahuatzin, you can't be the moon."

"¿Por qué no? Why not?"

"You're too short to be the moon!"

"Awww!" But nobody else volunteered.

He said, "Yo. ¡Yo quiero ser la luna!"

"Nanahuatzin, you can't be the moon!"

"¿Por qué no?

"You're too poor to be the moon."

"Awww!" Still, nobody volunteered.

"Voy a ser la luna."

"Nanahuatzin, you can't be the moon!"

"Why not?"

"You are too ugly to be the moon."

It was true. Nanahuatzin was short, Nanahuatzin was poor, and Nanahuatzin was ugly (Nanahuatzin actually means "face covered with festering boils"). Still, no one else volunteered.

Nanahuatzin stepped forward. Tecuziztequetatl stepped forward. Tecuziztequetatl made the first sacrifice. He took off his incredible headdress and threw those feathers right into the fire. The gods said, "Ohhh!"

Nanahuatzin had no headdress. He just pulled out a clump of his hair and threw that into the flame.

Tecuziztequetatl took off that incredible jade necklace and threw that into the flames. Nanahuatzin had no necklace. He took off his thin brown leather string he wore around his neck and threw that into the fire.

Tecuziztequetatl took off those incredible ankle shells, shook them, and threw them into the fire. The gods said, "Ohhh!" Nanahuatzin had no ankle shells. He didn't even have shoes, so he pricked his ear and dropped his very own blood into the flames.

Now the gods began to beat their drums, and they began to sing the sun and the moon songs. Tecuziztequetatl said, "Now you stay! I go first." He stepped up to the front of that flame—he was stunning in that firelight—and as he leaned into the fire, he became frightened. He leaned away from the fire.

Nanahuatzin looked up at Tecuziztequetatl. He stepped forward. Tecuziztequetatl said, "No! I'm just . . . I'm just getting ready. You stay." He stepped forward again, a second time, and a second time he stepped back. A third time he tried and got even closer—he put his toes into those hot coals—and a third time he stepped back.

Now the gods stopped singing and they stopped beating the drums. They looked on in disbelief and said, "Tecuziztequetatl is a coward!"

Tecuziztequetatl said, "I am not!" And he jumped very close to that fire, leaned in—it felt like his eyes were beginning to bubble and boil in his head—shook his head, leaned back, and hung his head in shame.

At this point, Nanahuatzin looked up at Tecuziztequetatl and felt bad for him. He looked at the fire. Gathering all the courage he had, he ran as fast as he could, jumped as high as his little legs could carry him, and landed right in the middle of the flame *y desapareció*. He disappeared in a shower of sparks. The gods couldn't believe it. They beat their drums again, even more loudly, and began to sing even stronger.

Tecuziztequetatl, taking courage from little Nana-huatzin, jumped into the flame too. Now the gods waited to see who would appear first in the sky—the sun or the moon. When Nanahuatzin was in the fire, he grabbed the hottest circle of fire which was the sun, not the moon, and rode the flames higher and higher into the air, all the way up into the sky. Tecuziztequetatl took what was left, which was the moon, the smaller, paler circle of fire that remained, and he carried it up into the sky.

The gods said, "It is as it should be. Nanahuatzin, even though you were short, poor, and ugly on Earth, in the sky you will be the brightest, most handsome thing. And Tecuziztequetatl, even though you were handsome and rich on Earth, in the sky you will be paler than the sun and not as beautiful."

But there was a problem. Tecuziztequetatl refused to move in the sky, and demanded that he and Nanahuatzin switch places.

Nanahuatzin did not move, and remained, still, and slightly smiling in the sky. Tecuziztequetatl refused to move. *Los dos estaban estáticos en el cielo* (they were static in the sky). One of the gods reached down and picked up a rabbit and threw it as hard as he could right at Tecuziztequetatl and caught him square in the face. Why a rabbit? I don't know, it's what the story says. The force of that rabbit being thrown from the Earth made Tecuziztequetatl, the moon, begin to move. Then another god reached down and picked up a huge boulder and threw it as hard as he could right at Nanahuatzin, but he was ready. He caught that boulder in a fiery hand, broke it into two huge pieces, threw one of those down back at the gods, and killed half of them with one blow.

To the other half he said, "I will not move until you sacrifice yourselves in the fire too." The other gods did. They jumped into the fire as well. Nanahuatzin then took the other half of the boulder and squeezed it into a million pieces of dust. They caught fire, and he flung them into the sky where they remain to this day as stars.

To this day, it looks as if the sun moves around the Earth and the moon follows behind. When the moon is full, look up to it and you might see what they see in Mexico. Here we see a man in the moon, but in Mexico they see a *conejo en la luna*. They see a rabbit in the moon. And now you know why.

La Virgen de Guadalupe

There was a native named Juan Diego who was a practicing Catholic. One day when he was walking back from church, just on the dusty slopes of the hills of Tepeyac not far outside of what is now Mexico City, he had a vision. He saw a beautiful woman floating on the back of an angel. She had rays of light going out from her. She had beautiful brown skin, just like Juan Diego. She looked at Juan Diego, and he fell on his knees.

She said to him in his native language of Nahuatl, "Juan Diego. Go to the bishop. Tell him that I am La Virgen de Guadalupe (the Virgin of Guadalupe) and I want a church built on this very spot where you are kneeling."

Juan Diego couldn't believe what he saw, and with that he went running back and stood in line for many hours until finally he got an audience with the bishop.

He said, "Bishop! I saw a vision of La Virgen de Guadalupe! She told me we need to build a church right there on the very spot where I saw her!"

The bishop looked at Juan Diego and knew Juan Diego to be a good man and a religious man, but still the bishop said, "Juan, I think that you should go home and get some rest tonight."

Juan left. The bishop didn't believe him. Juan walked home, and all week he had a heavy heart. The next week he went to church, and when he was leaving, halfway between the church and his home, on the same small rolling hill of Tepeyac, he saw La Virgen again. She said, "Juan, go back to the bishop and tell him that La Virgen de Guadalupe *demands* that a church be built on this very spot."

Juan went back and waited the many hours again for an audience with the bishop. The bishop came out, Juan told the story again, and the bishop said, "Juan, I'm beginning to think that there may be some truth to your story, but I can't be sure. Ask the virgin for a sign."

Juan Diego hung his head, walked home again, and had a heavy heart for the rest of the week. The next week he went to church again. After church, he was walking home when he saw the virgin in the same spot. He told

La Virgen, "Virgen! The bishop said that I need to bring a sign."

La Virgen de Guadalupe said, "Juan, right around the hill there is a bush of roses. Gather those roses up in your tilma (in your robe) and bring them to the bishop."

Well, Juan walked around to the hill and he thought, *Roses? In the middle of the desert? This is craziness!* But there, just like La Virgen said, bloomed a beautiful bush of the most amazing roses. He couldn't believe his eyes. He gathered up those roses in his tilma (his little brown robe), tied it carefully, and walked as quickly as he could back to the bishop. He waited for an audience with the bishop, and there, in front of the bishop, he said, "I've got a sign from La Virgen de Guadalupe."

Juan undid his tilma to spill the roses on to the floor, but nothing fell to the floor. Juan hung his head in shame. When he looked up, everyone gazed at his tilma while they were on their knees praying. Juan couldn't believe it. He followed the eyes of the bishop down to his tilma and right there, on his tilma, was a replica of La Virgen de Guadalupe, miraculously imprinted on the fabric, exactly as she appeared to Juan Diego in the hills.

With that, the bishop had his sign, they built a church for La Virgen, La Basilica de la Virgen de Guadalupe (the Basilica of the Virgin of Guadalupe), and they took Juan's tilma and hung it back behind the altar. If you go to Mexico City, you can get off the Metro train at the stop of the Basilica de la Virgen, and you can see that very same tilma. They say that four hundred years later it is still perfect. It looks exactly the way it looked when Juan saw La Virgen.

La Llorona

*W*hen I was younger, my mother would say to me, "Go to sleep or the boogie man will come and take you away." She never told me who the boogie man was, or why he would take me away, but when I was younger I believed her. In Mexico, there is no boogie man. In Mexico there is . . . La Llorona.

La Llorona travels along the rivers in Mexico looking for her children, and if she finds a boy who reminds her of her boy and a girl who reminds her of her girl, she gathers them into her thin, ghostly white arms, carries them under the water and holds them there for a year and a day. Then they slip from her grasp and wash up on the muddy banks of the river, another couple of victims of La Llorona. People will say, "They probably drowned." Others will say, "No, it's La Llorona."

If she doesn't find any children, she cries a terrible cry into the night sky, "¡Aiiiiiiiiiiiieeeeeee!" If you are brave enough to listen more closely, you might her say, "¡Donde están mis hiiiiiiiiijos! Where are my children?"

La Llorona means "the weeping woman," and there are many stories about why she cries and why she looks for her children. Some people say that her name was Maria, and she was an Aztec woman who married a Spaniard in the 1800s. They had two beautiful children, a boy and a girl, and he always promised to bring her and the children back to Spain with him when he left, but he didn't. One night, before his ship left, *ella se volvío loca*, she went crazy, and she grabbed her two children. She brought them down to the river and threw them in to get back at her husband. As she listened to her children struggling in the water, she realized what she had done, and she dove into the water after them, but it was too late. They slipped under the black water and were never seen again. She traveled up and down the river, crying, searching, until one day, too exhausted to go on, she slipped into the river, and she died.

The priest wouldn't give her a proper burial because of what she had done. They made a shallow grave near where she was found. Because of what she did, and because she didn't get a proper burial, she haunts the rivers in Mexico to this day, crying for her children.

The story varies in many ways. Some say she sent her children to the market one day and they slipped in the river and drowned. Others say her husband had an affair with another woman and she got back at him the only way she knew how. Others say she married the devil and when she saw her children developing horns, she threw them in the river.

There are stories of La Llorona that stretch all the way back to Hernán Cortés. Some say she existed even before Hernán Cortés. Hernán Cortés seduced a native woman as he was conquering the Aztecs in the early 1500s. She served not only as his lover, but as his spy and translator among the Aztecs. They called her *La Malinche*, which means "the tongue." After Cortés was victorious in his conquest, he cast her aside. They say that she recognized her betrayal of her people and has been crying for her people ever since. Another version of the story says that Cortés and La Malinche had two children together, and when he betrayed her and set sail for Spain, she watched the ships disembark from the shore, pleading with Cortés to return, if only for his children. He would not, and she slit their throats as the ships sailed away. Once the ships passed over the horizon, she realized what she had done. She came back to her senses and literally cried herself to death. She of course could find no rest, and so she searches the land, crying, looking for her children.

There are parallels with the Greek tragedy *Medea* written five thousand years ago. Medea gave up her homeland for love of Jason of the Argonauts, but when he took another wife who could make him a king, she avenged herself by killing their two children. This type of story became fact in the modern day United States when a woman named Susan Smith drowned her children in a lake because she was jealous of her husband's love for another woman. From Greek tragedy, to Aztec legend, to Mexican folklore, to modern day news, La Llorona seems to inhabit many forms.

Nowadays, the people of Mexico use the story of "La Llorona" to make their children behave. If their kids are upstairs not going to sleep, the parents will say, "You better go to sleep or La Llorona will come and take you away."

The little kids will say, "Okay, Mommy! We're going to sleep!"

When they get a little bit older, they're not quite sure if La Llorona exists. They'll be upstairs messing around, and their parents will say, "Do your homework."

"We don't wanna do our homework."

"Do your homework or La Llorona's going to take you away!"

The kids start doing their homework. They look at each other. "Hey, do you believe La Llorona will take us away if we don't do our homework?"

"Uh-uh. Do *you* believe La Llorona will take us away if we don't do our homework?"

"No way!"

"Why are we doing our homework then?"

"I don't know."

The kids will start messing around. At this point, one of the grandparents will sneak up the stairs, put his or her fingers on the door, and just barely open it so the kids see the door opening by itself, and the grandparent in the hallway will say, "Eeeeeeeee!!!"

The kids will say, "Mami? Papi? Tell La Llorona we're doing our homework!" They'll start doing their homework, and it works for the rest of the school year.

When the kids get to the seventh or eighth grade, they don't really believe in La Llorona anymore, but they love to tell the story at sleepovers and campfires, and they love to get their friends to jump with the story. One thing those kids also really like to do is to swim down by the river. Now, the river can be really wonderful to swim in, but it can also be really dangerous when the waters come down from the mountains.

If you dive into the river and you can't see a rock, you might hit your head and break your neck, or you might get your feet tangled in a branch, and then the current pushes you down and you drown. So for years and years parents have tried to keep the kids from swimming in the river when it's dangerous. They've put up fences. They've put up signs. The kids pulled the signs down and climbed over the fences, until one genius grandparent fifty or sixty years ago told the kids, "Hey, go swimming all you want, but if you feel fingers grabbing at your heels or fingernails digging in your shoulders, it's the last thing you'll ever feel because it's La Llorona pulling you down."

A few years back, when I was in Mexico, I heard that there was a sighting of La Llorona down by one of the rivers. I went down, and there were these four tough, teenage boys hanging at the edge of the water. They were daring each other to go in, but nobody went in. Finally one of the boys said, "I'm not scared. I'm going in." As he walked into that water, he put his toe in, but he must have stepped on one of those branches because he pulled his toe out like he stepped on something sharp, and we all jumped back.

Then we all laughed. The four tough, teenage boys went into the water, and all of the sudden on the other side of the river, a bush began to shake—and there was no wind! We heard, "Eeeehhhh!" We got scared. One of the kids turned to come out and we heard, "Eeehhhhh!!!"

We were almost ready to start running down the road when we heard, "Eeeehhh . . . hee hee hee!!!" And a little eight-year-old boy came tumbling out of the bush. He said, "I got you!" We got so mad! The one kid grabbed that little boy and dunked him like ten times. Every time he came up he said, "You thought it was La Llorona!" SPLASH! "You guys thought it was La Llorona!"

Afterwards, Miguel, the oldest teenager, said, "I know how you can see La Llorona. All you need to do is put a glass of water in your window, and she'll come up from the river and she'll drink it."

He said that he tried it on a Wednesday night at midnight. He put that glass of water in the window and he said, "Antonio. ¿Sabes que pasó? Do you know what happened?"

I said, "What?"

He said, "Nothing, but Thursday night at midnight, do you know what happened?"

I said, "What?"

He said, "Nothing. But Friday night at midnight, do you know what happened?"

I said, "Nothing?"

He said, "Wrong! Friday night at midnight, I remembered the America legend of Bloody Mary. I heard that in America if you go into the bathroom, shut the door, shut off the light, look into the mirror, and you say 'Bloody Mary' five times, she comes out of the mirror and she scratches you." He asked me if that was true.

I said, "Aw, yeah!"

I remember when I was younger, my cousin Julie told me about Bloody Mary. She came down from Boston when she was thirteen. I was about seven or eight.

She said, "Have you heard of the legend of Bloody Mary?"

I said, "What's that?"

She said, "Go into the bath . . . aw! You're too scared to do it."

"I'm not scared!"

"Yeah, you're a scaredy cat!"

"I'm not a scaredy cat! I'm gonna do it!"

I went into the bathroom, shut the door, shut out the light, looked into the mirror . . . too scared. I looked into the sink instead.

I said, "Bloody Mary, Bloody Mary, Bloody Mary, Bloody Mary, Bloody . . . Mary!" I looked up into the mirror. Know what I saw? My reflection.

"Ahhh!" I went running out. Julie said, "I knew you were a scaredy cat!"

She went in, shut the door, shut out the light. I put my ear to the door and listened. I heard, "Bloody Mary, Bloody Mary, Bloody Mary, Bloody Mary, Bloody Mary! Tony! Bloody Mary's got me!"

I said, "Oh no! What are you going to do?"

"Come in and save me!"

I said, "No way!"

She came out. Her arms were all scratched! She said, "Bloody Mary got me." I didn't go to the bathroom in my house for weeks after that. My mom made Julie call me on the phone and tell me she had made the whole thing up.

Well, anyway, Miguel told me he decided to mix the two legends and he said, "Antonio! Nunca mezcla dos leyendas." He said, "Never mix two legends," because he put that glass of water in his window, went into the bathroom, shut the door, shut out the light, looked into the mirror and said, "La Llorona, La Llorona, La Llorona, La Llorona, La Llorona."

When he came back the glass was still there, but he heard her voice across the yard. "Eeehhh!!!" He put four more glasses of water in the window, made sure they were full all the way up with water, went into the bathroom and said "La Llorona" as many times as he could stand it. When he came back, one of those glasses was gone. He put his back to the wall. The four glasses were above him on the window ledge. He looked around his room to see if his brother was there. He checked under the bed and looked in his closet. It wasn't his brother.

On the other side of that thin, brick wall he heard a sickening sound. It sounded like bones scraping brick, and he heard the sound of La Llorona drinking. He peered around the ledge just in time, and he saw her thin, bony hand pull down the fourth glass. This time he slid out from under the ledge and looked up at the three remaining glasses just as that bloated, disgusting hand with black, crusty fingernails pulled that third glass down. There were two glasses left, and as she grabbed that second glass, Miguel thought *I am going to prove that La Llorona exists.* He stood up, was eye-level with that glass, and waited for her to grab that glass, but she didn't. He began to think that he was imagining the whole thing when just then, that hand reached around that last glass and lingered there. It didn't move!

He said, "Now I'm gonna prove she exists!"

He took a deep breath, reached up, and just as he got close to that hand, it reached around and grabbed his hand and pulled him out the window, La Llorona looked him square in the eye, and with a horrible voice she said, "¡Tengo que ir al baño! I have to go to the bathroom!" And with that, she disappeared. "¡Eeeehhhh! ¡Mis hijos!"

Lake View High School

$\mathcal{I}$n my early career, I mostly told stories to children in elementary schools, and it seemed that I was well suited for it. I enjoyed it, the children enjoyed it, and the teachers and administration valued that I was entertaining while also promoting cross-cultural understanding and the value of being bilingual.

One day, I got a call from a middle school principal. She had heard that I was an up-and-coming storyteller, and would I consider telling at her school? She had three times the amount of money for an assembly than what I was used to making, and I eagerly accepted the invitation. As I hung up, I thought, "Telling stories to junior high school students? How hard could that be?"

When I got to the school, the principal pointed me to the gym. The students filed in morosely, sat down, crossed their arms, and stared at me. I started telling my sure-fire-never-fail stories, ones that children all over Chicago liked and teachers appreciated, and about 300 junior high students stared at me. Not a hint of laughter or even a smile at the funny parts, not a shred of understanding or nod of approval in the poignant parts, not a shiver or jump or even a blink during the scary stories. It was an unmitigated disaster. Nothing was working, the principal was sweating, and I felt like a drowning man at sea with a quickly deflating raft.

When I got to the last story I knew and I was met with the same stony silence, I looked at my watch, hoping this horror show was almost over. I was only supposed to tell for forty-five minutes, but when I looked at my watch, I was shocked to see I still had forty-two minutes to go.

Okay, that's a lie, but that's what it seemed like. When, mercifully, my time was up, not one of the students applauded. The principal started clapping, and a few students half-heartedly clapped with her.

As the students filed down off the bleachers, many of them passed me, and none of them would look at me. I realized, not only would I never perform in middle schools again, but the rest of my career was probably ruined too. One particularly tough kid sauntered by me and out of the corner of his mouth, barely audible, whispered to me, "Cool."

The principal's eyes got big, she came rushing over to me, and she said, "He hasn't said anything to anyone all year long! You are a genius! The kids have never been so quiet for an assembly! The last storyteller left here in tears! Can you come back tomorrow?"

I said, "No way!"

She said, "I've got the same amount of money for you."

I said, "Sign me up!"

Soon I began to tell stories in many other middle schools, nearly always with the same quiet, morose attention, and with offers to come back again as soon as I could. It wasn't long before I started telling stories in high schools too, and my first experience telling to high school students led to a dramatic, life-changing shift in my work as a storyteller. This is what happened.

After telling stories at Lake View High School on the north side of Chicago, not too far from Wrigley Stadium and just west of the lake, I was asked to teach an after-school storytelling and drama program. I worked there for three years. My first year, the kids told their own stories. The second year, we did mask and puppet work. My third year, they asked me to direct an actual play from a script. I chose the Greek tragedy *Antigone* because the story is about a teenager fighting for what she believes against a corrupt government that won't listen to her. She ends up dying for what she believes in, and society is ultimately changed. I asked the teachers, and they said, "These kids will never get it. They only read at 15 percent of the normal level. Why not try something easier, like *Guys and Dolls*?" At the drama club meeting, I told the kids what the teachers said, verbatim. I said, "I have never directed anything, never mind a Greek tragedy. So . . . you can't read, I can't direct, what've we got to lose?"

They said, "Nothing. Let's do it." I said, "I am going to treat you like professionals, and that means we have to memorize all the lines. We won't cut a single word." They said fine.

You probably know a little bit of the story of Antigone, but let me just explain it to you the way I explained it to those kids. You see, this is an ancient story, sort of a *telenovela* (a soap opera) of its day. There's a king who goes to a fortune teller who says his son is going to kill him and marry his mother. So he does the natural thing, he abandons the baby on a hillside.

The boy gets saved, is named Oedipus, and lo, he goes for a walk and runs into an old man who gets all salty and tells him to get out of his way. Oedipus says, with all due respect, forget you. The man acts all big, and Oedipus smokes him, you know, lays him out, kills the man in the road. He goes back to the kingdom and there is this woman, and she is fine. A lot older than he is, but she's fine fine fine, she's got it going ON. He's like, somebody slap me. She looks at him and says, Foxy, get your cute little self over here.

They get married. They kick it. Soon they have four babies, one of whom is called Antigone. So, things are all good, but then he goes to the fortune teller. Oops. He finds out the truth: you done killed your father and married your mother. He rips out his eyes and wanders as a beggar with Antigone and the other sister Ismene. Both the brothers want to be king, so they fight and kill each other, and in the power vacuum Creon, Oedipus's brother, steps in and he's like, I can run this thing.

It'd be like you walk outside, you see a Lexus with two dead people next to it and the keys in the car. Creon gets in and acts like it's his. But he's riding scared because who knows who's watching him in the hood. He decrees that the older brother be buried, but he passes a law that the younger brother shall not be buried, but left to rot in the street as an example to anyone else who tries to take power by force. Creon says that whoever tries to bury him will be killed. Antigone fights against this tyranny and buries her other brother despite the law. She gets caught. They talk. For twenty pages. Basically, Creon says just because you are going to marry my son Haemon, don't think that I won't have you put to death. Basically, Antigone says whoever is not buried wanders eternally, and I owe it to my brother to bury him. So she buries him. She gets killed. The boyfriend, Haemon, is so distraught that he commits suicide. Creon's wife kills herself. Creon buries everybody and rides his Lexus, all bummed out, and that is the story of Antigone.

The kids stared and then all started talking at the same time.

"I want to be Antigone!"

"I want to play the nurse!"

"When do we start? That stuff is dope!"

We have eight weeks to rehearse. Only problem, no boys show up. The girls are doing great, and finally they convince Alberto to join us. Alberto is one of the finest little freshmen, with flashing eyes and curly hair, a Puerto Rican Romeo.

He walks in and says, "I want to be the king. My girls tell me you need one."

I laugh. "Can you act?"

"Yeah, I can act, I can act good. Watch . . . 'What lig
in yonder window breaks, it is the east, and yo Juliet, s
is the sun.' Good huh?"

I say, "Sure. Can you memorize lines?"

"Yeah, give me anything, I'll memorize it."

"How about this speech (three pages of Creon)?"

"When?"

"Tomorrow."

"Okay. If I do this I can be the king, right?"

"Sure."

"You girls heard him, right? Cause I ain't going t
this work if I ain't going to be the king, and it's not like
got any choice in the matter anyway!"

We all laugh. He comes back the next day. Fully n
orized.

The girls lose their minds. One says, "Not only
but smart!"

We start acting out the play. We only really nee
more boy to play Haemon, the love interest. The girl
ing Antigone says she'll try to convince her boyfrien
next day there is a knock on the door. In walks Mai
toughest looking kid I have seen in a long time: 6' 2",
bald, chains, clothes, deep voice.

He says, "I hear you need a man up in here."

I say, "Yeah."

All the girls look at him. I give him the part of the lover, Haemon. Haemon, who is scared of standing up to his father Creon. Haemon who is crazy in love with Antigone. I don't have the heart to take the part from Alberto.

After a few days, Alberto stops rehearsal and says, "Yo. He should be Creon."

Marc says, "You sure?"

"Yeah, man, you're too ugly to be the lover. I should be the lover."

Marc laughs and becomes Creon, not as good with the lines as Alberto, but a powerful presence.

I went to rehearsal late one day, and my assistant Amy was turning around and around; there was mayhem in the auditorium. The kids were cowering in the chairs, Marc was standing on a chair on the stage raging.

"You stole my money. All y'all mothers. I'm going to smoke somebody."

Amy looked at me and said, "Thank God you're here! Finally an adult!"

Amy was three years older than I was. I walked up to the stage.

"Marc, what happened?"

He said, "I set my bag on the stage. I walked out to go to the bathroom. I came back, and my $50 was gone."

"I doubt anybody here took it Marc."

I look over my shoulder. Nobody says a thing.

He shouts, "Somebody in here stole my money!"

"Marc, would you ever set your bag down in the gym and leave it?"

"No."

"Or the cafeteria?"

"No."

"Or the hall way?"

"No."

"Then YOU messed up. You'll get your money." Amy and I and another teacher got $50 together.

When we gave it to him, he said, "Thanks. Now we can have our lights turned back on."

We spent three weeks trying to figure out the language and the characters, and a few weeks learning lines, and we got closer to opening when, one day, Alberto pulled me aside after rehearsal and asked if he could read me a poem. I said sure. It was about a boy who stood on the edge of a four-story building and thought about jumping off. The refrain was "will they even know I am gone?" I looked at him and realized that my whole life came down to this moment.

I said, "Alberto, are you the boy in the poem?"

He said, "Yes."

I said, "Alberto, it is a beautiful poem."

He looked at me and said, "I know." Alberto walked out of the building.

I sprinted down the hall and found the school counselor, and told him what had happened, and he ran out of the school after Alberto.

The next day the counselor met me and said that Alberto was in the hospital. When he saw my face, he quickly said Alberto was fine, but he *was* suicidal and had to be at the hospital under observation for a while.

Amy, my assistant, ended up playing all the boy parts, and two days before we opened, the cast was sullen, Amy frazzled, and the show a wreck. Then, like magic, Alberto walked in and said, "What's up!" He knew everybody's lines. We did the show opening night. The first half of it was amazing. About halfway through the middle of the twenty pages of Creon-Antigone, Marc started forgetting his lines, and at first it approached disaster, but then he began to improvise, like we talked about once early on in rehearsal, just in case of an extreme emergency.

This was an extreme emergency, and Marc said, "Uh, sit over here Antigone. Okay. Huh, how are you?"

"Fine. How are you, King Creon?"

"Good, good, it's all good. What you going to do later?"

"I think I'll bury the body again, King."

"Oh. How about after that?"

"Maybe die in a cave while my lover commits suicide."

"Oh."

Everybody on stage was laughing, everybody in the audience was laughing, and at the end, they got a standing ovation with the hard-nosed principal leading the way. This was the first play done in over twenty years at the school. Back stage, everybody was jumping up and down hugging each other.

I was so proud of them, and I walked over to Marc. He looked like he was laughing, his head down on the table. As I got closer, I realized he was crying, sobbing, his face a mess of tears.

He said, "I ruined the show. All that hard work, and I ruined it."

I had no words to console him. I said, "What do you want to do, Marc?"

He said, "Can you meet me tomorrow?"

I said, "Sure. When?"

"8:00 a.m?"

We worked all the next day, 8:00 a.m. to 4:00 p.m., and he got it, but we hid his lines all over the stage, just in case. The next night, Marc got through those lines, and the crowd gave them all a standing ovation.

Marc and the cast called me up to the stage, where he grabbed me in a great hug, holding me in the air. In that moment, I knew why I had been doing what I did in the schools.

He yelled, "What do we do next?"

I said, "Whatever you want."

Alberto said, "*Romeo and Juliet!*"

And Marc said, "Yeah, but this time, *I* get to be the lover!"

Faster than Sooner

I n the summer of 1997, I met two performance artists in Chicago. One was named Paul Turner. He grew up on a farm in southern Illinois. The other one was Donna J. Fulks. We began to write together, and we came up with a play called *The Hick, the Spic, and the Chick* .

I sent out cards inviting everybody I knew to come and see our play. We had a late-night venue on Friday and Saturday nights at 11:00 p.m. It was going to open in the summer, and we couldn't have been more excited about it.

I sent a card to my dad, and he called me up on the phone and left a message on my voicemail. He said, "¡Oye, Papito! Recibí su tarjeta que tu va a hacer un show que se llama *The Hick, the Chick and The Spic*. ¿Porque pusiste 'spic'? Porque tú no eres 'un spic'. Tú eres un Cubano. Tú eres bravo y fuerte." My dad asked me why I put "spic" in the title. I'm not a spic, I'm a Cuban, and I'm a tough Cuban at that.

I called my dad back on the phone. I told him that the play was going to be dealing with stereotypes, how people perceive us, and how we all wanted to challenge those stereotypes through humor and storytelling. Then I said, "Pa, I really want you to come see me in this play."

He said, "Mi'jo, de problem es, you know, es eh . . . eh . . . es I don't have too much money right now. You know, de flights are berry expensive from Delaware to Chicago, you know."

I said, "Well, Pa, I'm making a little money now. I'll send you a ticket and one for your new wife, Mary." I liked Mary very much.

My dad said, "Mi'jo, but de problem es, you know, es where are we gonna stay, you know? Your brother told me about your futon. I'm not gonna sleep in dat thing. No, no, no!"

I said, "Pa, I'll put you up at the Best Western Hotel," which is his favorite hotel for some reason.

He said, "Mi'jo, but de problem es, you know, es . . . eh . . . ees . . . I work all day Friday, you know. And Sunday morning I like to wake up, read the paper, take a nap, you know."

I said, "Well, Pa look. You gain an hour when you fly out to Chicago. You can go to bed early Friday night, see the show Saturday night. Sunday I'll buy you a *Tribune*. It's a great paper, and then you can go home and take a nap when you get home." In the background I heard his wife, Mary, say, "Come on, Honey. We should go."

He said, "Mi'jo? We'll see."

"Mi'jo" means "my son" or "my boy."

I wanted my dad to come see me because he had never seen me perform in all the years I'd been performing. I was hoping he'd come to closing weekend, which was in the middle of June. That closing weekend I had a storytelling in the morning at a local library. Then we were going to go to Chang's Invitational Tae Kwon Do Tournament. I'd been training for five years. Every year I would go to that tournament, and every year I would get knocked out. I figured my dad could watch me get knocked out. Then we would go to the Steppenwolf Theatre, where I was in the small studio space in a puppet show. For years we had tried to do our puppet shows at the famous Steppenwolf Theatre, and this was our big break. Then, at 11 p.m. that night, we were going to go to the Strawdog Theatre on the north side of Chicago near Wrigley Field and perform the play I had a hand in writing, *The Hick, the Spic, and the*

Chick. In one day, my father was going to see what I had been doing with my life for the past ten years. I was a little nervous about it.

When I was younger, my father would always tell my brothers and me the same thing whenever we got in trouble. Once we ran around in his office, and my dad from his desk said, "¡Mis hijos! Ven acá," and we knew we were in trouble. He came out holding a little wastepaper basket that little eight- or seven-year-old fingers had squeezed a whole tube of toothpaste into and smeared all around the edges.

He said, "You'd better tell me who did this. You better tell me who did this, but faster than sooner."

Now, whenever he messed up his English, we always started to giggle, which made him even more mad. He said "Ah, no, no, no . . . you better put the toothpaste back into the barn before I catch you a spanking."

At this point, we all were laughing, and my brother Henry had tears coming out of his eyes, he was laughing so hard. My dad threw that basket down, scooped up the three of us, took us into his little office, and threw us into his little leather chairs.

He said, "You . . . you . . . you better tell me but right now and NOT LATER!"

Whenever he yelled like that, we always started to cry. Then my dad said what he always said whenever we got in trouble and we started crying. He picked us up in his strong arms (our feet were dangling), and his beard scratched our soft cheeks. He said, "Mi'jos. Don't cry. Whatsamatter wid you? Men don't cry. I cannot wait until the three of you are mens. Then we sit down, you know, eat a nice filet mignon, drink a nice glass of cognac. But until then . . . don't cry!"

What my dad didn't know was that I already was a "mens." The year before, he had sat me down in that same office and told me that he couldn't live with my mother anymore because we lived so far away from work. He left, and I did the math that day, and realized that I was the oldest boy left in the house, which made me the man.

My dad was always teaching me how to be a man, but never quite finishing the lesson. I remember when I was five years old he taught me how to ride a bicycle. I was so excited. The day came for us to take off those little training wheels. We got the tools out of his perfectly ordered toolbox. Just as soon as we got the second training wheel off, my dad got beeped and had to go to the hospital. He's a doctor.

He said, "Aye, mi'jo. I'll ride you when I get back." He got into his car, but I was too excited. I couldn't wait. I got onto my bike and started riding. I was riding by myself. There was nobody on my street to share that with me. None of the neighbors were out, and my mom wasn't outside. It was just me and these leaves blowing up among the spokes. At the end of the street I fell over and skinned my knee and cried.

When I was eight, my dad taught me how to play baseball. My dad played semi-professional baseball in Cuba. He played with Tony Perez, who came to the United States and played for the Cincinnati Reds in the 1970s. He was a member of the "big red machine," you know? My dad took me out to the ball field; he put me on first base with a little glove. I'd like to say it was his old, leather glove from Cuba, but it was a plastic K-Mart thing he bought me.

He went to second base, and he said, "¡Mi'jo! Hold de glove like dis!" And he spread his hand out with the fingers wide in all directions. So I spread my hand out as wide as I could. He held that ball and he said, "Don't . . . move . . . de glove!" And he threw that ball as hard as he could. I didn't move the glove. The ball came and hit me right in the pocket. Not in the palm, where it stings, or in the web where it might come around and hit me in the face, but right in the pocket where the glove actually folds around the ball. I was so excited. I threw it back to him. He went way out to the left-field fence.

He said, "Mi'jo. Don't move de glove!" I held that glove, and he took that ball and threw it a hundred miles an hour. I couldn't do anything even if I wanted to. The ball exploded in my pocket and I caught it. I felt like I had won the World Series.

My dad held his arms in the air and yelled, "Dat's my boy!"

But he never taught me how to hit. I sat on the bench all through high school.

Every now and then my dad would say, "Do you want me to come to a game?"

I'd say, "Pa, I'm sitting on the bench."

He said, "I'll wait 'til you get in there, son." Secretly, I wanted him to come to the game anyway.

Once I really wanted to play catch with him. I woke up early in the morning before he went to work. I walked downstairs in my little Bionic Man pajamas and my little glove.

I said, "Pa, let's play catch today," and he said, "Mi'jo, I can't play catch today, but listen. I'll call your Uncle Tito. He'll come down. He'd love to play catch with you!"

I said, "Ah, great! Uncle Tito's going to play catch with me."

My dad went to work, and later on that day my Uncle Tito came to our house. We went outside, and he rolled the ball to me on the ground. I'd scoop up that grounder, throw it back at him, and he'd catch it, just like my dad, because he was a good baseball player too. After ten or twenty minutes of grounders I said, "Uncle Tito? Enough with the grounders. Why don't you throw me one in the air?"

"Okay, Papito."

He threw it on the ground again.

"No, no, really, Tito. My dad taught me how to catch. Throw it to me in the air!"

"Okay, Papito."

He threw it on the ground again.

"Tito, throw it to me like a man!"

"Okay, Papito!"

I held my glove just like my dad told me. Uncle Tito threw that ball. I didn't move the glove. He wasn't as perfect a thrower as my dad, so the ball came down and POP!

Smacked me right in the nose. Blood sprang all over my shirt. I started to cry.

Tito said, "Whatsamatter? Men don't cry! Whatsamatter with you?"

The last time all of us were together was on *La Noche Buena* or Christmas Eve. Christmas Eve is a huge deal for Cubans, and that night we had everybody . . . my grandmother Mimi, my Aunt Nina, Aunt Cachu, my Uncle Tito and Aunt Elia, my dad and stepmom, the three boys, my cousin Barbie, and my cousin Ray, who came in late. We had a huge pig on the table with the apple in its mouth and big blue eyes. My brother kept taking the apple out and saying, "¡Hola, Mimi!" out of the mouth of the pig. Mimi would say "¡Ay! Dios mio!" and she'd get really mad.

Ray started dancing the salsa around the table. There was grease everywhere and *tostones* and *arroz* and *frijoles* and *picadillo* and pig and water and milk and juice. It was incredible!

I knew enough to go for second helpings, and as I reached out to grab a spoonful of beans and rice, my grandmother leapt out of her chair, grabbed the spoon from me, and served me. She said in Spanish, "Men don't serve themselves. The women serve the men." For the rest of the meal, if I wanted more food, I had to wait until one of the women at the table served me.

Now that was confusing to me because on my mom's Irish side of the family, if you didn't serve yourself at the dinner table, you just didn't eat. I remember one time we were all together, and my mom cooked a big meal for us. As she was walking from the table she said, "You boys do those dishes now, okay?"

She walked out, and one of us in our adolescent testing phase said, "Ma, why don't *you* do those dishes?"

She froze in her tracks and said, "You want me to do those dishes?"

"Yeah, Ma. We want you to do those dishes."

"All right, I'll do those dishes."

She walked over to the kitchen table, put both hands on one side of the table, swept them straight across and smashed every dish against the wall. She said, "The dishes are done!"

We jumped up, cleaned the whole kitchen, vacuumed her room, washed the car, and everything.

I watched how my father adored the women in the house, and yet, I saw how he seemed to take advantage of them. I was already trying to figure out what made the most sense for me from both cultures.

One of the most important gifts my dad gave me was the gift of my college education. While it was part of my parents' divorce agreement that my dad had to pay for my college education, it also was his American dream to send his children to college. He did this proudly and generously, showing me that a man takes care of his children, even through a bitter divorce.

After four years of college, I called my dad and said, "Pa, I want you to come to my graduation."

He said, "Mi'jo . . . the problem is . . . "

I interrupted, "Pa, there's no problem. You paid for this education. I want you there."

He said, "Mi'jo, is your mother gonna be there?"

I said, "Yeah, Pa, but with 8,000 other people. There's a ton of people graduating."

He said, "Mi'jo, listen. I . . . when you get back to Delaware, I take you out, okay? I'll be with you in spirit."

My dad didn't come to graduation, but he did take me out when I went back to Delaware. He took me to the Hotel DuPont Restaurant, the most famous restaurant in all of Delaware. We had a special table up in the back. There was a harp player not too far away. We had a thick filet mignon. Afterward they brought out these two wonderful cognacs. My dad took the snifter, rolled it around, and sniffed it. I did the same. I tasted it, and it tasted horrible, but I wanted to be just like my dad.

Afterward he looked me and said, "Ay, Niño, I have had fantasies about this moment. Now you are a man. Papito? Tell me. What do you want to do with your life?"

I said, "Pa, I want to go to graduate school."

"Mi'jo, more school? More money? That's okay. That's good. You want to go to business school?"

I said, "No, I don't want to go to business school."

He said, "They make a lot of money, you know. You want to go to law school?"

I said, "Pa, no. I took a law class and I liked it, but I don't want to go to law school."

"Thanks be to God because I HATE the lawyers!"

Then my dad got all misty-eyed and he said, "Mi hijo, you want to go to medical school? Ay, niño, I have fantasies of you being a doctor with me some day, Son. You know, we have our little beepers on, walking down the hallway, you know. And you beep me, I beep you, you know . . . eh? I pick up de phone, I say, 'this is Dr. Sacre. No, no . . . the sexy one!'" It was my dad's favorite joke that night. He told it four times.

I said, "Ha, Pa . . . very funny." After the laughter settled down, I said, "Pa, no. I don't want to go to medical school." Then my dad got confused.

"Mi hijo, business, law, medical . . . what else is there, Papito?"

I said, "Pa, I want to go to acting school."

My dad put that cognac down, looked at me, held his finger up in the air and shook it to the left and the right, a nearly universal Cuban sign for 'not a chance in the world.'

Then he said, "Not with my money."

That was the most important lesson he could have taught me, because I moved to Chicago in 1990 with my own money, a hundred dollars and a credit card some fool gave me in college. I became a fantastically successful actor. Well actually, I never quite made it as an actor, but I did make it as a storyteller. It's a blessing and the love of my life. It's my calling. I love to tell stories to kids, and I love to tell them to go home and talk to their parents about where they came from and why they came from that place and what they're doing and what it was like when they were younger. But I've never really done that with my dad. I've made up stories about how he came from Cuba, but I've never really asked him.

Every year, after the Oscars, my dad calls me on the phone at 6:30 in the morning. He says, "Mi'jo," and we have the identical conversation each time. It changes very little every year.

"Did you see de Oscars last night, Son? Ay, I have fantasies of you being up there someday, you know? You be holding that little statue, you know, and you look so good in your tuxedo, you know? The camera cuts to me—I look even better—then you look out into de camera and you thank me."

After dinner one night, during one of my frequent visits to see my dad, he got his car keys and he said, "Mi'jo, let's go for a ride."

Mary, my stepmom, got up to go with us, but he said, "No, Mary. I want to have a ride with my son. I want to talk to my son tonight," and he gave me the car keys. He never does that, so I knew it was a big deal. Anyway, I drove and looked at him through the corner of my eye.

He said, "Papito, what do you want to do five years from now?"

I said, "Pa, I want to be telling stories. When I look out at all these kids, it's incredible. Their eyes are so big, and they run up to you afterward and share their stories..."

He pointed to a gas station and yelled, "Papito! We should put gas there. That's a good place to put gas. We go there tomorrow, okay?"

I was confused as to why he so quickly interrupted me, and I said, "Okay, Pa, we'll get gas there tomorrow."

"But, mi'jo, the kids, storytelling. That's good, but what do you really want to be doing, Papito?"

"Well, I want to continue working with these masks, these puppets. I mean, people actually believe they come to life, you should see the people in the theater!"

He pointed out the window to a restaurant we were passing, and again, shouted, "Papito! That's a good place to eat lunch! We should eat there, Okay, Papito?"

"Yeah, Pa, we'll eat lunch there tomorrow."

"But, mi'jo . . . the kids, the puppets . . . what do you really want to be doing, Papito?"

"Well, I run this after-school drama program at the high school. The kids trust me with their stories, and I want to continue teaching the drama . . ."

"Papito! What's that right there?"

"What, Pa?"

"There!" he yelled, pointing to a light on the dashboard.

"Pa, that's the windshield wiper fluid. We need to put in more windshield wiper fluid."

"Papito, we'd better do that . . ."

"Okay, Pa, we'll put in more windshield wiper fluid."

"But Papito, what are you really going to be . . ."

"You know, Pa, in five years, I'm gonna win an Oscar."

"Ay, mi hijo. That's what I like to hear. That's my boy!"

Well, closing night came for *The Hick, the Chick, and the Spic* and my dad didn't come, but that night the artistic director of the theater spoke to us and said that based on the reviews and the crowds we were getting, he wanted to extend the show all summer long. We extended for two and a half months. All of a sudden people were coming from everywhere to see the show. It was sold out almost every night. It was the hottest ticket in Chicago that summer.

I called my dad and said, "Dad, we are closing Labor Day weekend. You gotta make it that weekend. No excuses."

My dad said, "Mi hijo, the problem es . . ."

He had a conference to go to. As we got closer to Labor Day weekend, a woman from the cable channel Home

Box Office called. She wanted to see if our show could possibly be filmed and aired on her network.

I called my dad and said, "You have one more chance. Please come." I didn't check my phone machine for the rest of the week. Paul and Donna, the "hick" and the "chick," and I sat backstage and heard all the people filling up that space, wondering if the HBO person really was going to come or not. We came out of those curtains, and there was the HBO woman right in the middle of the theater. And there, in the front row, was my dad and his wife, Mary, and my two horrified brothers.

Paul and Donna did their pieces, and the whole time I didn't think once about the HBO woman. I thought I was going to do the piece that I had written, the piece you just read, in front of my dad? And, in honestly one of the most courageous moments of my life, I told the story, all of it, of my dad trying to teach me to be a man and not quite finishing the lesson.

When I got to the end, I said, "My dad didn't come to see the show all summer long, but tonight, he did. He's sitting right there in the front row." I pointed to him, and a stunned silence came over the audience. My dad stood up, and he'll tell you he didn't know what to do, whether to laugh or cry, but he turned to the audience, and he held up both fists in the air and shook them once.

Then some girl in the back said, "He *is* the sexy one!" Everyone started laughing, and he came onto the stage and gave me this great, big, real hug, not the typical Cuban hug with the pounding on the back, but a real hug. While everyone was clapping and laughing, my dad whispered in my ear.

He said, "Mi'jo. Tonight was *better* than an Oscar."

How Do You Say Blueberry in Spanish?

When my son was an infant, my wife and I talked to him all the time. She spoke and sang to him in English, and I spoke and sang to him in Spanish. With each passing month, we wondered when he would speak, what his first word would be, and what language it would be in. Would it be "Mommy" or "Papá?" Would it be *cat* or *gato*? He seemed to be progressing normally, and right around one year old, he spoke his first word: "Bah!"

"What did he just say?"

My wife said, "It sounds like he said, 'Bah.'"

Well, it wasn't quite English or Spanish, but at least it was a fully formed, recognizable syllable, and we knew that once a baby could begin to enunciate syllables, speech couldn't be far behind. It was cute. He would point to the cat and say, "Bah." He'd point to his mommy and say, "Bah!" He'd point to the car and say, "Bah."

After a few more weeks, he still only said "Bah." I was a little concerned. My mom said I didn't say much until I was almost three, but that when I did start speaking, it was in full sentences. I had some fun with it. When our good friend and neighbor Catherine, a teacher in the local schools, visited one afternoon, she asked if he was speaking yet. I said, "Sure, watch this." I turned to my son.

"What do baseball players play with?"

He said, "Bah!"

I said, "That's right, a ball! What does mommy give you before you go to bed?"

"Bah!"

"That's right, a bath! What's the opposite of good?"

"Bah!"

"What's on the other side of your chest?"

"Bah!"

"What's Scrooge's favorite word?"

"Bah!"

"What's the chemical symbol for Barium?"

"Bah!"

"What difficult exam do lawyers need to pass?"

"Bah!"

"He's a genius."

But after she left and we put our son to sleep, I had a serious talk with my wife. Were we doing the right thing? She was convinced that we should raise him bilingually, and she said it would just take time. I intellectually knew this—heck, I even made a career by being bilingual—but emotionally I was torn. What if he was already falling behind?

We decided we would continue the path we had discussed of talking to him in both languages, at least until our next visit with the pediatrician.

At our next visit, Dr. George wasn't concerned. He said our son was developing normally. He was adamant that we continue to raise him bilingually. He said there is much research that says bilingual children not only can communicate with more people, but their brains are actually stronger at many other tasks as well, including problem solving.

There, in the doctor's office, with our baby son anxious to get back to doing what babies do, sleeping and eating, it was what we needed to hear. "Continue to raise him in two languages." Doctor's orders, and I was relieved.

Not too long after that visit, our son began to speak! His actual first word was "ball," clear as day, and it felt like over the next few weeks he learned many words.

Some words were in Spanish, some were in English, and we were thrilled. Every time he said, "Ball," I would say, "Pelota." Ball, one syllable, *pelota* three, but I would repeat it and repeat it until he got it down.

He would say, "Thanks!" (one syllable). I'd say, "Gracias." (three syllables).

He'd say "Peach!" (one). I'd say, "Melocotón" (four). I'd say it over and over until he got it.

He'd say, "Fire Truck" (two). I'd say, "Camión de los bomberos" (eight). He'd look at me, perplexed.

He'd say, "Blueberry!" (three). I'd say, "Variedad de los arándanos azules" (Thirteen. Thirteen? Are you kidding me?).

Why, oh why does my father's tongue need thirteen syllables to say *blueberry*? But I don't give up, because some words are so beautiful in Spanish. The way my dad says, "Mi tesoro, mi alma, mi vida, mi corazón" when he talks about my son, his grandson, is so touching. It basically means, "Sweetie" but sounds like poetry in Spanish.

The specificity of the English language is wonderful. We have raspberries and strawberries and blackberries and boysenberries and cranberries, and in Spanish, they are all just *bayas* or berries.

We've made some mistakes along the way, some that have lodged into our own particular vernacular. For example, I walked with my son one day, and my little beeper on my watch alarm sounded. My son said, "Qué es?" I didn't know how to say "watch alarm beeper," and as I searched my brain for how to say that, I said, "suena la campana."

A few weeks later, we were with my dad, and my watch chimed again. My son said, "Suena la campana, abuelo."

My dad started laughing.

"What?" I said.

"It's hard to translate exactly, but what your son said was 'the bell tolls for thee'!"

Now, for anything that remotely sounds like a bell or an alarm, my son and I say in Spanish, "The bell tolls for thee," and we both laugh. My dad has even given my son his first of many Cuban nicknames he will have in his life, "La campana," the Bell.

Now we are looking at schools for him. I have traveled all over, and I have seen firsthand how wonderful dual language programs are. The children I meet in these schools have perfect accents in English and in Spanish. The famous research team of Thomas and Collier states that children raised and taught in two languages have scores that typically lag in their early years and then leap over the scores of their monolingual peers by about fifth grade, in all subjects, not just language, echoing what Dr. George said.

We have decided that dual language is the path for us. However, there is no dual language program in our neighborhood of Los Angeles, and the ones that are available in other districts are incredibly competitive, with often two- to three-year waiting lists.

We mentioned this to Catherine, our neighbor, and she told us that the fact that he is already a fluent Spanish speaker means that there is no waiting list for him in those districts, and makes it more likely he will get into the program.

However, she's a public school teacher, and her mission is to increase attendance at our local school. When she saw how important it was to us, she marched down to the principal's office and asked her to consider adding dual language to the school. It never occurred to me to ask for this, and I was so inspired that a neighbor would be moved to make sure that all of us in our neighborhood had a chance to enjoy the benefits of dual language.

Will the dual class come to fruition? We are not sure, but we forge on, trying our best to do the best we can for our child. *Centavo a centavo, se llena el saco*, penny by penny, we fill the sack.

We Stand Together

*W*hen I first met high school English teacher Mr. Dennis Danziger (or Mr. D to his students), I was surprised by his intelligent eyes, his caring face, and his size. He was at least 6' 5", and I blurted out, "Man, you are tall. Do you play basketball?"

"I did. My coach in college told me if I were a little faster, a little stronger, had a better shot, a better dribble, and better defense, I'd be on the bench in the pros. So close, and yet so far. But here I am, living the dream."

I started laughing. He had such an ease about him. He was a teacher at Venice High School in the Los Angeles Unified School District, and he wanted to discuss the possibility of my doing a writing residency in his twelfth grade classroom.

I was excited to learn that he had received a grant from an organization called PEN in the Classroom. He thought I could help his students find their stories, and afterwards, PEN would publish those stories in an anthology. He thought the fact that I spoke Spanish would be a wonderful gift to his bilingual students.

I instantly liked the man. The money wasn't that great, however, and I told him so.

He said that many of his students had so much potential, and so many people had already given up on them. He taught some of the poorest kids in the Los Angeles Unified School District, and yet they still were in school, battling to graduate.

I was moved by his passion for his kids. We continued to talk, and he told me that before teaching, he was a writer for a big TV show that was probably before my time. He was making all kinds of money, living the Hollywood dream. I asked him, "What TV show?"

He said, "Taxi."

I said, "Oh my goodness . . . "

"Yeah, it was kind of a big show . . . "

"No, I mean yes, it was a big show, it's just, man, you are old, old, old, but ancient old, you must be a senior SENIOR citizen. I mean, that show was on in black-and-white, right? How old *are* you?"

He laughed, "Thanks a lot. You're not so young yourself. I see that gray in your hair. I was young when I had that job. And I gave it all up to teach these students. I wouldn't trade it for the world."

I was intrigued. Here was a man who had turned down a life of wealth to become a teacher, with all of the pressure and none of the wealth, to serve some of the poorest, most challenging students in one of the most challenging school districts in the country, and yet he seemed very happy.

He took my silence as a sign of my reluctance to work with him.

"I know the money is not great, but tell you what, I'll take us out to lunch before every class, my treat. It's a great sandwich shop, and I'll throw in a copy of my new book. Final offer."

He held out his hand, and I shook it.

"I'm in, but lunch better be good, and your book better not suck."

He said, "I know lunch will be good, and if my book doesn't make you laugh at least once, I'll give you your money back."

I said, "But you're giving it to me."

"Exactly."

I laughed, and we walked out towards his car. He opened up his trunk and pulled a book from a cardboard box. He handed it to me. As soon as I read the title, I started laughing.

He said, "I told you. One laugh, guaranteed."

It was called *A Short History of a Tall Jew*. I read it all in three sittings and laughed out loud often.

When I first walked in his classroom a few weeks later, I instantly saw how much the students respected Mr. D, and how much they distrusted me. We had decided at our lunch meeting that I would start with my stories about being raised in two languages, and how I gave up my first language, and how relearning it led to my career as a storyteller and a writer.

No story I told them elicited any response. They mostly listened, and they sort of watched, but they didn't react. No laughter, no questions, just stares. One kid (he had to be a gangbanger for sure, piercings, bald, black clothes, tattoos) sat in the back and looked at me, hard. One kid texted under his desk the whole time. Another never opened his eyes. I was humbled, excited, and ready for the challenge, but it was going to be a long, hard slog, for sure.

After class, Mr. D told me how brilliant I was, how he'd never seen the kids so quiet and attentive. I didn't believe him, but somehow, he gave me confidence for our next session.

At our weekly lunch before session number two, he told me about the many nationalities represented in his class: thirty kids from twenty countries, and the many different types of students: athletic, poor, rich, disabled, and so on. We laughed a lot while eating the best sandwich in Venice in the warm California winter sun. He, a Jewish teacher, I, a Cuban-Irish-American storyteller, both old as dirt to these teenagers. But we had one common goal: to help the students write stories and poems so that PEN could publish them as an anthology and the students could see their words in print. I had two months. Could I do it? Could I inspire them to write enough to fill a book? Would the stories be any good? Could Mr. D help me help them? Was I too old, too out-of-touch, not cool enough to reach these kids? What the heck was I doing in that classroom?

My hope was to help them open up to their own stories by hearing my stories. But after another class of some of my sure-fire, never-fail stories . . . nothing but stares. Nothing worked. I said, "Maybe it's time for you to tell some of your own stories?"

Nothing. The bell rang, and they nearly sprinted toward the door, none of them looking at me as they left.

Two sessions into it, and I wasn't sure this was going to work out. At the next lunch, I told Mr. D this, and he told me that he would see what he could do.

Mr. D cajoled, begged, pleaded, yelled, joked with the students. While they laughed with him, when he turned the class over to me and sat down at his desk . . . nothing. We were at an impasse. The only sound was the seagulls screeching outside the window, on their way to the beach, a mile and a whole world away.

Finally, I said, "Look, you have an opportunity to get your stories published, to get them out into the world, but I can't make you, and I've told you all the stories I know. I'm going to shut up and listen. Anybody who wants to talk, you step up to the podium, you talk, just tell me one sentence or two of what you think the story might be that you will include in our anthology, and I am willing to sit here in uncomfortable silence for as long as it takes."

It took a long, long time. The longest five minutes of my performing/teaching life. Mr. D said nothing, and I said nothing, and then finally Courtney stood up. She wore braids off the side of her head and a shirt with a cute kitten on the front that made her look very young, but her eyes and her furrowed brow made her look oddly like an old woman who had seen too much sadness.

She spoke just above a whisper, and the class leaned forward as she said, "I left my home in upstate Washington 'cause my mom was a mess, I don't want to tell you what she was into, but I got on a bus and stepped off it in Venice. I live on my own, work at the grocery store, and am a straight A student."

Nobody said a word, and she sat down.

I waited. Mr. D waited. The sea gulls screeched.

The Japanese kid stood at the podium. "I'm not sure if any of my extended family survived the tsunami. We can't get through to them."

An even deeper silence fell over the room. He sat down and put his head on the desk.

We waited.

A thin kid with wispy hair stood up and said, "They call me guero, meaning blondey or whitey. But they don't know that I'm 100 percent Mexican. But Mexicans think I'm too white, and white people think I'm too Mexican. I don't fit in anywhere."

We waited.

The bald gangbanger kid in the corner stood up. I tried not to flinch. I don't think I did. Maybe I did. I don't know. He was scary. He . . . sauntered to the podium, and turned around.

He glared at us. He opened his mouth, and in the sweetest voice said, "It's not easy keeping this head so clean and smooth."

There was a stunned silence, and then thirty kids from twenty countries and two old dudes just started laughing and laughing and laughing, and he stroked his smooth baldness and sat back down, everyone high-fiving him on his way back.

And now, the floodgates were opened, and kids could barely keep in their seats. They were leaping at the podium, looking for the chance to tell just one sentence of their story. I just sat in stunned amazement, and after each story, the kids would clap and cheer for each other, and I said nothing, not wanting to influence—even worse, prevent—this incredible flood of emotion and strength and vulnerability. I didn't want it to end.

The bell rang at the end of class, and nobody moved. The bald kid said, "Man, we barely got started."

We waited. I didn't want to break the spell.

And Mr D said, "*That* is what I'm talking about. We barely got started, and we have seven more weeks to get these stories out and on paper. This guy will be here," he pointed at me, "and I'll be here, and that podium will be here. You go to fifth period, and read chapter 5 tonight. All of it, you scallywags."

Those kids left, and Mr. D walked over to me and held out his hand. I shook it. He smiled, leaned close, and said, "Took you long enough."

Together, thirty kids from twenty nations and two old-as-hell dudes created an anthology of stories called *I Stand Alone*. On my best days, I think that if we can create that, we can do anything. I don't always feel that way, but when I do, it's powerful. This is my letter, my letter to those students, included as a final entry in their book of writing.

For Mr. Danzinger's Venice High School Seniors (and Courtney, a Junior)

I came to Venice High School to work a two-month writing residency with questions: Would Mr. Danzinger be as cool of a teacher as he seemed to be outside of school? Would I be able to find the office through the maze of slow-walking, jean-clad, texting teenagers? Is this really where they filmed *Fast Times at Ridgemont High*? Then I walked into the classroom with more questions: Would I be too nervous to tell my stories to seniors ready to graduate? Would they listen? Can I really help them write anything? Is that kid white or Mexican? Will that gangbanger in the corner kill me? And how does he get his head so shiny and bald? It's so smooth. I wonder how he shaves it.

And then, you read one sentence of what your story might be and you started talking, and listening to each other, and I had more questions: Do they have the courage to face their wounds and put them on the page? When will that kid stop texting? Does that kid ever speak out loud in this class? How did that girl get the gumption to leave home and pay her own rent? I know people twice her age who can't do that, and she's in school, to boot. Why did that girl lose a grand-pop-pop so young? What did that bastard do that to that girl? How did that girl make it here from Bangkok? Did that kid lose anyone in the tsunami? Will that gangbanger in the corner kill me, and *how does he get his head so shiny and bald*? It's so smooth. And shiny.

And you wrote, and rewrote, and stood up here, at this podium, with the recycling piling up on the counter, those seagulls blaring, constant knocking on the door, people walking in and out,

and you started:

to pour forth,

erupt up,

drizzle down,

gush over, scream whispers, speak secrets, reveal wonder, show courage, rip tides, tear veins, spill silliness, flood eyes and break

hearts

OPEN, revealing wonder, revealing wonder, revealing wonder.

Making me laugh, making me sigh, making it hard for me to keep my eyes dry,

so I witness, and scribble in my journal as you speak one powerful, wrenching, funny story after another,

knowing I couldn't take away the pain of what some of you have survived, knowing I couldn't touch the vibrant life and strength that all of you possess,

and how do I say to all of you

you have a survival skill set so strong

cause you are here, now, in class,

not dead or in jail or ditching,

you are *here*

and it doesn't feel like it's anything big to you but I know it's *amazing*.

How can I convince José that he doesn't stand alone,

that he stands with me

He stands with me

You stand with me

I stand with you, behind you,

Carrying your memory to audiences all over this country,

I'll rewrite this scribbled jumble of words sixteen times, polish it,

and tell it,

and tell it,

and journey with you although we may never see each other again,

After we bring forth this book into the world,

We stood together, for a time,

We stand together, we stand together,

and although I have more questions, always more questions,

at least I have one answer,

the answer we've all been searching for, and here it is . . .

For a shiny head, all you need is Neutrogena, and a Mach 3 razor, and lots and lots of aftershave.

LARRY SERGEANT

When I first started storytelling, I had a teacher who told me he believed that storytelling could save the world. My first reaction was like, "Okay. Whatever." But when I thought about it, I began to realize that it made some sense because if you know somebody's story, it's harder to hate that person. If I know your story, you become like a brother or sister to me, and if you become like a brother or sister to me, I'm going to fight for you. Really hard.

When I was in the fourth grade, the class bully was named Larry Sergeant. He was held back two years because he was so stupid (or that's what everybody thought). One day we were at recess and we were playing kickball. Larry was picking on Binky Minor, the smallest kid in the class. Larry was like 5'10" and Binky was like 4' 11". It just looked so silly.

Now, Larry had shoved or kicked or tripped or mocked or flicked or smacked or humiliated just about everyone in the class, and it was just Binky's turn, but something that day made me step between them. I looked up at Larry and I said, "Larry, you should pick on someone your own size!"

Everyone stopped playing, all eyes turned to me, and all of the sudden I got sort of full of all that attention. I said, "Yeah! You should pick on someone your own size!"

Larry looked down at me and said, "Okay" and picked me up like the beanpole that I was and slammed me to the ground.

I said, "Ow!!!"

All of the air went out of my body. When that air finally came back, I said the worst thing that I could think of: "You jerky jerky jerk jerk!"

We started hitting each other, and just then the teachers came and broke it up, and we got major detentions. Major detention meant that that day after school we had to sit in the classroom, look out the window for sixty minutes, and think about what we had done.

I sat after school and looked out the window and thought, *I am a hero. I stood up to the class bully (even though I got my butt kicked).*

Larry was also looking out the window, and I saw that he was starting to cry. Just one little tear, but it was enough, and I thought, *Ahhh. Larry's a sissy. I can't wait to tell everybody Larry's crying!*

Then I looked and saw that he started to sob, big heaves that made his huge shoulders go up and down, and I said, "Larry. What? What's wrong?"

He said, "This is my fifth major detention. It means now I get kicked out of school."

I thought, *Yeah! I got the class bully kicked out of school. Yeah!*

He saw my smile and said, "That means my dad is gonna beat me up."

I said, "Wait a minute—you mean you're just gonna get grounded? That happens to me when I get in trouble."

He said, "Uh uh. My dad's gonna hit me in my face with his fists, then keep me out of school until my bruises heal, then he's gonna put me in another school. That's why I'm so far behind in school."

I was so ashamed that I was the one to send Larry home to a beating from his father. If I had that moment on the playground again I would not have picked a fight with Larry. He did get kicked out of school, and I never saw him again.

What he was doing was wrong, and it's quite possible that he was going to get kicked out of school anyway.

The older I get, the more I think about what my teacher said. I don't know if storytelling can save the world, but I do know that if I knew Larry's story, then it would have been impossible for me to hate him.

MY DAD IS THE MAN

*W*hen my dad's family left Cuba in 1960, conditions were very bad. In 1994, conditions in Cuba were so bad that thousands of families all left Cuba at once. A lot of them couldn't afford to come over in planes or boats, so they made rafts called *balsas*. The rafts were made of inner tube tires, wood, plastic, chicken wire, and anything they could get their hands on. It was a very dangerous journey.

I went to Miami to talk to some of those *balseros*— the rafters who made that long journey to America—to ask them what their voyage was like, why they left Cuba, and especially what stories they were telling in Cuba since 1960 when my family left. They shared with me some of their songs and stories, so I decided to interview my own family as well. Maybe there were some stories still waiting to be uncovered.

I sat my Uncle Tito down and I asked him about his journey. I told him how I was telling my friends how my father swam over from Cuba and he laughed. Then he looked at me and said, "Do you know how your father came to America?"

I said, "Yeah. He came over in a plane."

He said, "No. Mimi, your grandfather, me, your aunts, and your cousins all flew over to Miami. Your father, like many other young Cubans, was forced to be a soldier in Castro's army. Your father spoke out against Castro's army, and one day your father's best friend came running into the barracks and he said, "Ñico! Tu tienes que salir porque ya vienen los fusilados de Castro!" He said, "You'd better leave right now because the firing squad is coming from Castro to get you!"

My dad, without grabbing anything, without saying good-bye to anyone, leapt out of the window, ran into the woods, and stayed in the woods all night and all the next day. Then, under the cover of darkness, he escaped to the Peruvian Embassy. The Peruvians flew my dad from Havana to Miami.

I looked at my Uncle Tito, and I thanked him for telling me that because now I know the truth, and I can tell my friends that my father stole five planes from Castro's air force . . . no! He stole *twenty* planes, a whole battalion of planes, from Castro's air force and flew families all over the . . . he stole an aircraft carrier from Castro's navy and saved thousands of people and then . . . no! He was the man who stopped the Cuban Missile Crisis, brought down the Berlin wall, and he is the man who stopped communism all over the world. My dad has . . . he did a bunch of other things! Really, he did! My dad is the man, and that is the truth! ¡*La verdad*!

Hacerín, hacerado, este cuento se ha acabado, y el tuyo ya está empezando, que sea más salado.

A literal translation might be: Snip-snap-snout, this tale's told out, and yours is just beginning, make sure it is saltier!

It basically means, "The End," but like so many other things, it sounds much better in Spanish.

About the Author

Antonio Sacre, born in Boston to a Cuban father and an Irish-American mother, is an internationally touring storyteller, author, and solo performance artist based in Los Angeles. He earned a BA in English from Boston College and an MA in Theater Arts from Northwestern University. He has been a featured storyteller at the Kennedy Center, the National Storytelling Festival, the National Book Festival at the Library of Congress, and museums, schools, libraries, and festivals worldwide. His books and recordings have won numerous national awards, and he is the author- and storyteller-in-residence at the Lab School on the UCLA campus.

Website: www.antoniosacre.com
Facebook: www.facebook.com/antoniosacreauthor
Twitter: @antoniosacre
Pinterest: http://www.pinterest.com/antoniosacre/

About Familius

Welcome to a place where mothers are celebrated, not compared. Where heart is at the center of our families, and family at the center of our homes. Where boo boos are still kissed, cake beaters are still licked, and mistakes are still okay. Welcome to a place where books—and family—are beautiful. Familius: a book publisher dedicated to helping families be happy.

Familius was founded in 2012 with the intent to align the founders' love of publishing and family with the digital publishing renaissance which occurred simultaneous with the Great Recession. The founders believe that the traditional family is the basic unit of society, and that a society is only as strong as the families that create it.

Familius' mission is to help families be happy. We invite you to participate with us in strengthening your family by being part of the Familius family. Go to www.familius.com to subscribe and receive information about our books, articles, and videos.

Website: www.familius.com
Facebook: www.facebook.com/paterfamilius
Twitter: @familiustalk, @paterfamilius1
Pinterest: www.pinterest.com/familius